D1043371

Kim
Stay Strong
Stay Brave
Be Bold!

from Beaten to Badass

MY JOURNEY OF BROKEN BLESSINGS AND
HOW I BECAME MY OWN HERO

ERIN BAER

Positively Powered Publications
Louisville, CO
PositivelyPoweredPublications.com

Cover Design: Melody Christian
Project Editor: Amy Collette
Proofreading Editor: Alexandra O'Connell

FROM BEATEN TO BADASS / Erin Baer—1st ed.

Library of Congress Control Number:2019914543

ISBN: 978-1-7329022-9-9

Praise for *From Beaten to Badass*

"I am a domestic abuse survivor. Those words had always been difficult for me to say. After reading *From Beaten to Badass* by Erin Baer, I now find healing in those words. Erin is a survivor of life. She found her identity, purpose, and hope in all that is good. Her story is a must read, showing that someday, as survivors, we can stand tall in our own presence.

– Monica Duran

"Erin is a force to be reckoned with! She is fierce, passionate, courageous, relatable, and has a powerful story to share. Erin articulates how lessons in life don't knock you down, but rather build you up, create your purpose, and ultimately ignite the badass that resides in us all. Her voice is commanding, and while her experiences are heartwrenching, they are a call to action to build ourselves up and step into the individuals we were created to be. *From Beaten to Badass* will bring you to tears, trigger your inner power, and ultimately should be shared with anyone who's been knocked down and needs to borrow someone else's strength to get back up!"

– Lauren Danielle

"*From Beaten to Badass* is the heroic tale that all women need in their lives. Whether you've personally gone through domestic or sexual violence yourself, know someone who has, or have never seen the damage that these traumas can leave behind, you need to read this story. Erin's strength is beyond comprehension, and her determination and spirit are so inspiring and uplifting. *From Beaten to Badass* is the true story of a warrior."

– K. Hanks

"Are you feeling trapped? Overwhelmed by aspects of your life? Read this book, and get started on your journey to a more positive you. Life is tough and it can hurt, but Erin has faced what has been thrown at her with amazing resilience. She was knocked down time and time again but always came back stronger. This book is a testament to her inner strength."

– Peggy

"Erin has an amazing way of making the lessons she's learned throughout her life resonate with her audience. She is not only an incredible author but she provides guidance and makes you feel like you're on the journey with her, learning from her experiences."

– Juliana

“I sincerely want to thank you for writing this and having the courage to do so when others such as myself are too ashamed or embarrassed to write it publicly. You are a warrior and a Badass.”

– Kate

“I LOVED this book! The author, Erin Baer, shared her powerful story acknowledging her own personal experience with abuse. Her story from self-recognition, to ‘now what?’ then to rise above and succeed is so inspiring. Resetting the mind from ones ‘tipping point,’ *From Beaten to Badass* is a must read!”

– Sofia

Every woman needs to read this book and then *re-read* it. Erin Baer engages the reader and motivates the Badass in all of us. Her vulnerability in her story touched my soul. I felt like she put words to how I felt and what I myself went through. Her journey has inspired me and I am confident it will inspire so many.

– Carla Castillo

Dedication

To those who find hope, strength, and inspiration
within my story to become true heroes of their own.
May you become the Badass
you were always meant to be.

Quit saying no to yourself.
Start saying yes to yourself first.
— Erin Baer

Why the Elephant?

Elephants have always been my favorite animal. The majestic yet giant creature shows such strength and power in all of its wonder. Yet, in their size they are sensitive, wise, stable, intelligent, loyal, peaceful, reliable, and determined in all that they do. I feel a connection to the qualities that the elephant has and only hope to be as majestic while living a life of integrity and confronting the "elephants in the room."

Elephants also never forget, as I have never forgotten. I continue to move forward, learning from my past, embracing my present, and looking toward my future with the patience that these gentle giants possess.

~*Erin Baer*

Table of Contents

Foreword

This is a book written for women who have ever experienced the hoot, holler, cat call and inappropriate comments made as we pass by men we don't even know. In other words, this book is written for all women. Too many girls and women accept the uncomfortableness of those situations and ignore their own feelings, telling themselves, "It's not a big deal, don't be so dramatic," "I should be flattered," "He's just drunk," "Maybe I shouldn't have worn this dress," etc. The messages we receive as to how we should accept those inappropriate behaviors set us up to make excuses for intimate partner abuse.

Erin tells us that "If you only look at things one way, you limit your ability to overcome obstacles and problems with different solutions." *From Beaten to Badass* shows us how she was able to overcome her obstacles and live a life she deserves.

As we have become enlightened with the Me Too movement, it's time to stop asking, "Why doesn't she just leave?" and instead start asking, "Why is he allowed to continue to do that?" As I write this, I am working with a woman who is the fifth wife of an abusive man. People should be asking, "How is he able to get away with this abuse over and over again?" But everywhere she turns, people are questioning her behavior. It's so easy to be on the outside and only see the black and white (or in some cases, black and blue) and not see how grey things really are. When a person grows up with abuse, as Erin did, it wires their brain differently. Add manipulation, gaslighting, and coercion, and you create something very murky and difficult to see.

Like many of my clients, Erin was never exposed to the red flags of abuse, and it came as a shock when she confronted the idea that she "allowed" herself to get into it. "How did I let this happen?" is a common way to feel. Especially for women who are independent, educated, have careers, and outwardly appear to be strong. Erin questioned her behavior and actions and felt crazy. How was she to know she was experiencing gaslighting? Then she tried to make sense of everything. But how do you make sense of someone hurting you and then bringing you red roses and professing their love? You do it by believing there must be something wrong with you.

As Erin saw when she looked into the mirror, you start to not even recognize yourself. Humiliation is a powerful feeling that is very effective in maintaining control over another person. It often takes a "tipping point" before someone says, "No more." Erin acknowledges that she was lucky enough to have people along the way who stood by her. It is my experience that it's nearly impossible to get out of an abusive relationship without the help of at least one other person. That might sound simple, but there are women who have been isolated and beat down so low that they have no one.

Fortunately, Erin is a fighter who didn't let her flame burn out, and she has people, past and present, who made all the difference. As she has taken the steps to recover, she has learned that by raising her voice she not only lifts herself up, but many others.

Thank you, Erin, for telling your story and sharing your voice so that others may find theirs as well. Thank you for being the badass that you are and for being the example for so many who need a shining light to follow. The Urban dictionary states that "the badass carves her own path." You have done that and are showing us all how to find our inner strength.

—Diane Wall, LPC, Psychotherapist and Executive Director of Zero Tolerance For Domestic Abuse (0T4DA), which provides counseling, education, and awareness for domestic abuse

Introduction

Be patient, put in the work, and you will be amazed at the outcome. –Erin Baer

At first glance, I seem to have it all together. Life is good. But it hasn't always been that way. My story has many peaks and valleys, twists and turns with good, bad and ugly parts. However, I am blessed in every sense of the word.

I am going to share the most intimate parts that defined my life. Some are good, some are absolutely terrifying, and others are life-defining. Regardless, they are the moments that make up my story, my truth, my life.

The seeds in our lives are planted when we hear something, whether it is from parents or teachers or friends, bullies, bosses, or coworkers. Seeds are the way we are treated or how we are defined by those people. It's up to us whether we plant them by believing and nurturing those seeds, or we throw them aside and say, "That's not true. That's not who I am. I will nurture the seeds that fall in line with my life or the life I want to live."

Beaten

Some of those seeds make us feel like we've been beaten down by life, whether it was in school, at work, or abuse by parents, bullies, or by beating ourselves up. Some of those seeds are traumas we have survived, such as illness, grief, or infertility that knocks us down; anything that's beaten us down in life.

Badass

But we can still get up. Circumstances don't have to define us. We can make the choice to live the life that we want to live regardless of what's happened in the past. That's a decision we have to make.

I want you to know that you are not the only one who has been through it, whether it was being bullied as a kid, or abuse growing up or in relationships. If you're like me, you started believing that you weren't good enough or what you did didn't seem good enough.

No matter how hard you've been beaten down you can still be a badass, because it's already in you. You just have to make the choice to be that badass yourself. Your scars are beautiful. They don't define you, they just show you the roadmap to your true passion. What God intended you to do. You are beautifully broken.

When I've told my story, some people say, "Oh my gosh. I'm so sorry you went through that," or "That has to suck," or "Don't you wish your life was easier?"

Well, yeah, it sucks that I went through that, but at the same time I feel that God picked me to be the person to show others on a similar path the way.

Your circumstances don't define you — you define you. Therefore, just because all of this happened to you doesn't make you a bad person; it doesn't make you weak, it doesn't make you a victim. I feel that you can be the victor of your own life if you choose to be.

It never seemed like I had any other option but to be optimistic and positive.

If you have ever tried to tell your story, it is way more complicated than you would initially think. In the past I attempted to justify my life or excuse it for what it is due to specific people and/or circumstances. However, I ultimately came to realize that it is all a broken blessing in many disguises, and if I take 100 percent responsibility, then I can change it.

Les Brown, the motivational speaker, says, "When life knocks you down, try to land on your back. Because if you can look up, you can get up. Let your reason get you back up."

No matter what I was beaten down by: bullying, abandonment, sexual assault, domestic violence, and so much other stuff… I had been beaten down but it didn't matter because I kept getting up.

What I am about to share is my own view from the top of the mountain.

As a woman of faith, I truly believe that God put specific people in my life to help guide me on my journey while small interruptions came up. I view interruptions as anything that caused my journey to slow down, be halted or thrown off track. In my life, I have had many.

The people in my story are not just people. They are parents, friends, teachers, coaches, and mentors who embraced me, taught me lessons, and armed me with the necessary tools for life.

Ultimately, I became my own hero: a strong, independent woman who possesses qualities that are a perfect match for what life throws my way.

Through it all, I gained self-insight and resilience while I traveled through peaks and valleys, with the help of so many that made a difference in my life. My journey of fortitude enabled me to find who I was meant to be, as if it were there all along. You will learn about these influencers and the lessons they taught me while also learning about my many personal life experiences.

Growing up wasn't easy for me, but I didn't know any different.

Sometimes

April 1, 2010

Sometimes Life gets you down
Sometimes Life turns you around
Sometimes Life is everything
And sometimes Life is nothing

Breaths are taken
Chances are given
Memories are made
and some forgotten

You have a choice
Float on through
or reach for the sky

CHAPTER 1

Laying the Foundation

Focus on one moment, so that all the moments can be seen in the big picture. –Erin Baer

LIFE UNEXPECTED

May 27, 2001

Life unexpected
and without warning
is graceful and filling
nicely unplanned and amazingly
surprising

Hopeful, thoughtful, and wonderful
Yet there are those moments of doubt
slivers of seconds that are mind numbing

time where pain sets in and fears arise
where you must indicate the individuality of yourself
as your performance ascends to grace or falls behind

You must remain fully present
or where you thought your feet were planted
roots may cripple and fruits may rot
and end in a cataclysmic state

You can remain secretive
and stay consistently indulged
in the fretful place
or you can choose to secure yourself in the love of others
yet they themselves are the navigator of their vessel
and must choose the future destination

So, become transparent
within your soul –
follow thy heart and live your journey and you will find
your paradise

My life started out like everyone else's. My parents met, fell in love and wanted children. The only difference was that I entered this world with a twin sister.

My parents were together for about three years, until one day he came home to find my mother and us twins gone. He waited long into the night. The next morning came and went. He called friends and family, but we were nowhere to be found. His nightmare became reality; his life crumbled.

My mother, my twin sister and I eventually ended up in Kansas City. Our mother met a man and had another child. Now we were one happy family, right? Not for me.

For as long as I can remember, I was always different. I didn't look like the other girls, talk like the other girls, and I just marched to the beat of my own drum. Growing up without any friends was my normal but I didn't understand why. I just knew kids didn't like me. They found me annoying and ugly. And when they did pay attention to me, they were picking on me. I was the underdog and the one no one wanted around. It wasn't like I didn't try to make friends or be included; I did. Eventually I grew tired of it. I was the kid who didn't play at recess and instead went around saving anthills and using my imagination to disappear in my own mind, waiting for the bell to ring.

I was the kid who was well-behaved, shy, and didn't speak up. I was the kid who stayed to herself, sat in the front of the class; the one with perfect attendance, and the one who focused on just surviving the day.

I was also the kid who got taken out of language arts and sent to speech class because I had trouble pronouncing my S's and Z's. The class was fun, but the teasing because of it was terrible. I never spoke up in class, I didn't want to read out loud, and I did my best to do well. If I didn't understand something, I wouldn't raise my hand; I was frightened to death. I hated school. I loved learning; it was everything else I despised. I just wanted to be liked and when that didn't happen, I just wanted to disappear into the background. I stayed quiet, I slouched in my seat, and the teachers took notice. They did their best to tell me I was a good kid and that there was nothing wrong with me.

But when you're a kid and *no one*, absolutely no one your own age likes you, you question your very existence. Questioning, *What is so wrong with me that not even one kid likes me?* I was skinny and short with crooked, bucked teeth and big gums. Can you picture it? I was called Mr. Ed. Yes, the horse, Mr. Ed! It was awful. When I was in first grade, all my hair was cut super short. I looked like a boy! My mother tried to help me gain self-confidence and she also enrolled me into Taekwondo. I loved it! The teachers I had were wonderful. They did their best to encourage me, even sending hand-written notes home. I grabbed a hold of that small gesture. Those handwritten notes were worth their weight in gold. They gave me the encouragement I needed to face another day in school and focus on my studies. I took pride in my work.

I kept striving to make my teachers proud because if I made them proud, maybe one day I would make others proud, and then hopefully I could make myself proud.

I started gaining more confidence in my school work and that's what I began putting all my focus on. Seeing how proud my teachers were of my school work gave me the strength to keep doing my best academically. The pats on the back were my motivation to keep showing up to school, even though I knew the day would end with tear-filled eyes because of how the kids treated me. Finally, the school day would end and it would be time to go home. Not that that was any better.

By the time I got off the bus and started up my long driveway home, tears would be rolling down my face. Some days Mom would be home to greet us and ask how our day went. Growing up with a popular twin sister was hard. Many would suspect it was simple and delightful, but I was more alone than you could ever imagine.

As my sister went on about how wonderful her day was and all the fun she had, I would sit in silence and wait. My answer was always the same; my day was horrible. Kids teased me and left me abandoned at lunch. No one wanted to be around me. The conversation always ended with me just wanting to be alone. Not only was school unbearable, so was the bus ride home. I did my best to avoid the kids and stay to myself. I was constantly picked on, getting pushed out of seats and then in trouble for standing up in the aisle, even though I had no other choice. One year I almost got kicked off the bus for standing up so often. Well, thank goodness the bus driver, Charlie, knew I was a good kid and let me sit behind him where he could see me at all times. That was a blessing and a curse. A blessing because I was safe from the physical torment, yet a curse because I was teased even more because I was considered a "bad kid" by the others. I just wanted to make it home and find safety within my imagination.

At this young age is when I started to have an entrepreneurial mindset. I began learning about the planet and how cool it was (and to me, still is). I was so driven to help and save our planet that I started the Reduce, Reuse, Recycle initiative in my school. With the help of my mom, who was also passionate about the Earth, we were able to bring in a musician who sang about Earth and how we can help her survive. My love for our planet allowed me to focus on something rather than stew in loneliness and self-pity. But, goodness, did I get teased. I didn't care, though. I felt I was helping our planet. I even wrote a letter to our world letting it know that I really enjoyed how it turns and how the stars twinkle at night.

It didn't end there. I required my family to start recycling and composting. My stepdad and I would go to the recycling center and turn in our aluminum cans and glass bottles, which back then was a big deal because you could make money. However, the little spirit in me made sure that money wasn't going to be spent on just anything, but to buy trees to plant. I remember when we had finally saved up enough to buy three trees, one for me and one for each of my sisters. We planted them down in the garden in the back yard. I took great pride in my tree. I made sure that I gave it water and I would visit it. I wanted my tree to know I wasn't going to abandon it and I cared about it. I felt that if I showed my tree love, it would do its best to thrive and grow. It was a symbol of life to me. I guess you could say I was sentimental. Anything I did that seemed pure, raw and just good, I held onto. I made those visits to my tree purposeful in my own way. Only one tree survived of the three trees that were planted; that tree was mine. I am happy to report that it still stands today.

My schoolteachers obviously took a liking to me; they saw something that I didn't and gave me special responsibilities. I liked my teachers; they made me feel special.

Who would have known that a foundation was being laid purposefully to tell stories and become a published author 30 years later? It really is quite remarkable. I never realized it, but I have always been an author. My first work was published in *Student Contributions*, the school's paper, when I was in third grade.

Funny thing is, I don't remember all of the things I did well, except for my handwriting. I was constantly complimented on it from my teachers and that in itself is amazing, because I am left-handed. Some may be confused about why that would be amazing in itself, but if you're left-handed you'll understand completely. Yes, I was teased for that. However, I take great pride in my handwriting because Mrs. Haney and the teachers that followed made sure to always tell me how beautiful it was. That meant the world to me.

I didn't have anyone I could really talk to, so for me writing was an outlet. It was a friendship I had with pen and paper. Reading some of the things I wrote brings sadness to my heart. All the things that people teased me about, I really liked about myself. I wrote about it; I wrote about how I loved myself and that I liked being left-handed. I also talked about my wishes for fame, how I liked going to the gym, how I looked good in a bathing suit.

The more attention and praise I received from my teachers, the more the kids didn't like me and the worse the bullying became. Kids began calling me teacher's pet, suck up, brownnoser and many more awful things. It was terrible. Yet, it didn't stop me from working hard. It's all I had, to keep the teachers happy because it was my sun on all my rainy days.

LESSON OF ACCEPTANCE

My Mother

My mother was young when she met my father (who was 25 years her senior) and they fell in love. As luck would have it, my mom wanted children and she conceived with not just one but two children: twins. I am not a mom yet, but I can only imagine that when a woman finally births her first child it must be a magical moment.

My mother had no idea she was pregnant with twins, she just assumed there was one and that she had gained the appropriate amount of pregnancy weight. When she went into labor, the doctor performed a C-section. I was the first to arrive.

Once I was taken to the cleaning station, the doctor announced, "There's at least one more!" My mother's reaction: "At least?" And in fact, there was at least one more, my fraternal twin sister. To both my father and mother's relief the "...at least one more!" announcement was in fact just one, and not more.

Mom had to quickly wrap her head around the idea that not only did she just become a mother, but a mother of two. I cannot imagine what that must have been like, but it must have been overwhelming.

As I grew up, to my parents I was Erin, but to the world I was grouped along with my sister who entered this world two minutes after me as "the twins." I am not saying it was a bad thing, but it got old really quickly as we entered into school. Before that we were sisters, but in school we were the twins.

Our mother did her best to encourage everyone to treat us differently, as we were different. The one thing we had in common besides the obvious (parents, siblings, etc.) was our birthday. But to me, though we celebrated our birthday on the same day, I was and will remain two minutes older. My sister can never catch up unless I die before she does. (That was meant to be funny!)

However, once we did enter our school years, being treated equally became impossible when it came to our peers and it became quite apparent to me that I was in for a long lesson of acceptance.

Acceptance is quite the task. Have you ever looked up the word? The Oxford English Dictionary definitions are as follows:

Acceptance –

1. The process or fact of being received as adequate, valid, or suitable.
2. Willingness to tolerate a difficult or unpleasant situation.

As children, we don't know the word "accept" and its meaning, but a word we do know is *like*. We know what that means and we know how it feels. Therefore, as a child our word for acceptance was like in present tense as well as past. The word like is simple, it is easily understood, and it makes sense to a child. That child being me.

As grade school progressed and my twin sister was being accepted by our peers, I was sitting alone at recess, during lunch, and in the classroom. I created a mindset that I was not being accepted and no one liked me. I couldn't figure it out. *Why was my twin sister liked by everyone else, but I wasn't?*

Did she only like me because I was her sister or was there something wrong with me? Was she only pretending to like me because she had to, because she was my twin? Was I not enough? What was it exactly? To this day I can't tell you why those kids were so mean. I was bullied, picked on, teased, and left alone day in and day out consistently by the kids I went to school with. It was very lonely.

Way back then in the 1980s, we didn't have internet or cell phones, so when I got dropped off by the bus at home and had to walk up our long driveway in the country, I was safe. Safe at home, with my twin sister, my little sister, my mom and my stepfather and our pets. Sounds wonderful, right? Well, living in the country was quite wonderful, because for me, being in nature was peaceful and I was left to myself, with my thoughts and my creativity.

Now, you're probably wondering, "What does this all have to do with your mother and how she taught you acceptance?"

Everything!

How we are treated at home, at school, and everywhere in between creates a cornerstone of how we view the world, relationships, and most importantly, ourselves.

I constantly questioned my acceptance both at home and at school. School was rough, and home became no different. I wasn't bullied, teased, or pushed around at home, but I was pushed aside.

The way my twin and I were treated was very different in the sense of our acceptance. The only way I can explain it is due to our very different outlook and personalities. After all, we are two very different people.

I considered it a good thing that we were treated as individuals and it was, until I became ignored almost everywhere.

There was a contrast in the way we were treated even though we were twins. I was shy, while my sister was everyone's best friend and loved attention. I did my best to stay clear of attention, stay to myself, and just survive the day.

At home, my twin sister was just as admired as she was at school, where I seemed to disappear into the background. My bedtime was at eight o'clock and hers was at nine. I woke up early and ready with energy, while my sister was a late sleeper and grouchy to the point you just left her alone.

She had friends and I had to tag along just so she could go, even though I didn't want to go as much as her friends didn't want me to be there. She was invited to sleepovers while I stayed home organizing my room. She did ballet and tap, while I did gymnastics. She liked to sing, I liked to draw. She liked to read, I liked to be outside in nature. She loved to run, I loved to golf.

It became very apparent that my sister had much in common with our mother. They bonded, and during the school year I was left on my own to figure life out. My mother and twin sister had a bond like no other. They were in a club all their own.

I couldn't break into that club even if I wanted to, and I soon figured out there was no point. I just wouldn't be accepted. I decided it would be best to stay out of the way and make myself as invisible as possible.

My mother did her best to help me gain self-confidence and try to accept myself growing up. She put me in therapy, signed me up for Taekwondo (the only activity we did together until she viewed me as her competition) and just kept telling me, "Sweetie, one day this will all make sense, but for now just hang in there." She would buy me self-help books for kids, tell me to look in the mirror and repeat "I like myself" 10 times every morning, but it just wasn't enough for me and especially for her. The only thing that helped was growing up, but I wasn't there yet.

Back then and to this day, I remind my mother too much of my father. Remember all those things that made me very different from my twin? Well, many of them came from my father, especially my love for golf. Plus, I look very much like him, so I am sure that didn't help.

My only saving grace was summer break. Year after year, I would look forward to my summers, because it meant I could get a little taste of what acceptance felt like, what being liked meant, and what having friends could be. My summers were the best! It meant I got to go visit my dad in sunny California and spend my days at Verdugo Hills Golf Course.

It was pure joy. Verdugo was my safe place because it's where I felt belonged and accepted. My summers were like dreams that lasted for two months at a time where I could be me, where I didn't have to worry about being pushed aside or treated differently, because I was me and that was enough. The summers defined who I was and gave me hope in who I could become. I was paid attention to by my dad and my friends at Verdugo, and I was able to spend time on the golf course, which taught me lessons I will never forget. My sister joined me at Dad's a few times, but eventually she stopped and it was just me and my dad, hanging out with our buddies at Verdugo, playing golf, doing fun things, and learning about life. That is what gave me hope to keep fighting for me.

Summers were dreams I never wanted to end, but they did, every July. However, while they lasted, they were magical.

I had hope that each new school year would be different, a new start, but each time it failed me and I had to endure yet another tough year of being bullied, teased, pushed around, pushed aside and not accepted for nine long months.

As school would start, I braced myself for another year of hell, but held on to the sweet smell of the golf course, the view of the mountains and the acceptance of my friends in California.

My school years were tough and the only times I enjoyed school were at recess when I could swing high into the sky, or protect the anthills from the trampling feet of kids, or sit and talk to the teachers who gave a damn about me.

Science and art classes were my favorite; I could explore different worlds in science and express myself with judgment-free creativity in art. Well, that only lasted a few years until I made a homemade gift for my mom on Christmas that I called the Can Man.

My mother had always told me that handmade gifts were the best, better than anything you could buy at the store. So, at the age of 10 I remembered this. I was determined to make the best gift for my mom that Christmas. She would always say, "Make your gifts honey, they will always be beautiful to me."

I had this dancing flower doll that I loved. It was purple and had sunglasses, and played music on a guitar. I thought if I made a gift for my mother, she would be happy, especially if I took one of her favorite things (Coca Cola) and one of my favorite things and put them together. I found the most perfect empty Coca-Cola can and washed it, making sure it was absolutely pristine.

I then took the flower doll I loved so much and tore it apart, and created what I called the Can Man. I spent lots of effort and time on this beautiful Can Man and I loved it! I was so excited to wrap it up with a beautiful bow and give it to my mom for Christmas.

Christmas morning came and gifts were being opened. I was smiling from ear to ear when I gave my mom her gift. She opened the package carefully, took out the Can Man, looked at it, looked at me, then told me it was the worst gift she had ever received. She hated it! My mom took that gift and right in front of me, threw it in the trash. It broke my heart.

I decided at that point I should never create again. A few years went by and I remembered that moment on Christmas morning; I didn't want to ever feel that pain. I took art classes, drew when I had to draw, painted when I had to paint, but never wanted to create a personal gift again. I would keep my own drawings to myself, hidden away in my own sketchbooks in hopes they would never be found by anyone.

The moment that my 10-year-old self-witnessed such disgust from my mother when I gave her a handmade gift, the Can Man, sent a very powerful message. Not only did my mom crush my creativity, but the messages I received were of unacceptance and not being good enough.

Everybody gives us seeds, and it is our choice whether or not we take those seeds, plant them and nurture them. You see, that 10-year-old little girl inside of me took the seed of her mother taking that Can Man and crushing it and putting it in the trash as: *I'm not good enough, and nothing I create will ever be good enough.* It took me many years to understand that only the seeds I decide to plant myself are the ones that are important.

I learned a powerful lesson of acceptance from my mother, in many aspects of the word. Just from that one incident, I began to believe that I wasn't good enough. Not only did the kids at school not accept me, but I felt my own mother didn't as well.

Remembering that moment that cut so deeply really defines my relationship with my mother. I didn't realize it back then, but looking back, it makes complete sense to me now. I have always sought her approval and acceptance. After all, she was my mom. I was always seeking her permission to be who I was, rather than just being me and being encouraged by her. As an adult, I never understood why my mother treated me the way she did; the pain, the damage she caused was deep. I sometimes wonder what it would have been like to be accepted or encouraged by anyone, especially my own mother. Would I have blossomed sooner? Would I have thought differently about myself? Would I have ever questioned her love for me? I guess I will never know. I had to figure out how to show myself the love, kindness, and encouragement I so desperately wanted rather than rely on it from my mother. It never changed my desire to seek it. However, it just made it more painful with every urge I had to fill that hole, the hole within my heart that my mother was supposed to fit in.

It wasn't until years later that I grasped the true lesson of acceptance from my mother. She had a tough life, beyond what I know and more than I can imagine. I had heard bits and pieces of it growing up, but only to the point that I can conclude she did the best she could with the hand she was dealt.

As a mother you are to love your children unconditionally and never abandon them. She had a hard time expressing unconditional love, but I am ultimately accepting of it. The times she abandoned me were when I needed her most and when guidance and support was more important to me than ever.

I will never understand her reasons for abandoning me. Maybe they are justifiable, but it's not for me to decide. What I can tell you is in those moments when she left me to fend for myself, I gained self-love, acceptance and strength.

She has taught me to accept all people and their faults, including mine and hers. For that, I am forever accepting of myself and who I am, and I do forgive her with a grateful heart for the lesson of acceptance, a priceless lesson at best.

Years later, we discussed the Can Man incident. I was shocked she even remembered and in even more disbelief about what she told me. These are her words regarding the biggest lesson she learned, which ultimately taught me the lesson of acceptance.

"Your Can Man will haunt me forever! He taught me a great deal over the years. If I had just said 'wonderful,' you would have felt better, but I was a jerk and couldn't see how much time you put into it. The very question of my entire life: what is time? I remember the Can Man above all gifts I have ever received… Ever. He is within my thoughts and dreams. He is a constant companion and reminder to really see. A lesson for all good moms with all good children giving good gifts. To see past how much 'time' something took, to look at the love and to give the recognition of it back. To applaud their creative tries and inspirations! To not walk into the shadow. The Can Man is one of my truest life lessons."

Those words from my mother echo through my soul and are more than enough of an apology for me, for everything I have ever questioned, from the whys to the how could yous. She did the best she could; she loved me the only way she knew how and she gave me the greatest gifts she could give me: life and a life of acceptance, a true broken blessing.

It is not my responsibility to push blame on my mother nor is it my duty to point fingers at her. She did enough of that for herself through the lesson I so unknowingly taught her with the gift of the Can Man.

The Can Man will be the thing that defines so much for me, as it does for my mom. I used to be hurt, disappointed, and quick to get angry at her for all the things I felt she did wrong, rather than be thankful for all the things she taught me through the times I felt she made mistakes.

Mom, you were the right one to teach me more than you'll ever know. You made mistakes, yes, but so did I. That is the broken blessing in all of this because to me, beyond any explanation, you taught me one of the greatest lessons that many, unfortunately, never learn. You taught me the acceptance of not only others, but of myself and who I am and how I matter. What life throws my way – as long as I stay true to myself, I will survive.

LESSON OF STRENGTH

My Father

April 18, 2000

A man who's always taken
Life for what it's worth
Proud of his accomplishments
Understands his mistakes

Doesn't show emotion allows it to hide
Takes care of what needs to be done
Shows concern when necessary
A man who's sure of himself
Happy with a true meaning
Not just another guy
Has his own personality
Understanding of anything
Stubborn at times
Believes a lot is taken for granted by the youth
An honest soul
Has a warm heart
Not scared for what is to come
Appreciates everything because it's not just given
Listens to who needs guidance
Has never been mad at mistakes I have made
Accepts me for me
Proud of how I've run my life
He's proud to call me his daughter
And a man I am proud to call my Father
Chan Bush

I have always put my father on a pedestal, leaned on him — but that isn't fair. Eventually, I brought him back down to earth and that showed me where true strength lies. We are impeccably close and I feel extremely blessed to have him as my dad. From the moment I came into this world my dad and I have had an unbreakable bond.

I have always known without a doubt that he loves me and that he has my back no matter what. I am definitely my father's daughter.

I learned a great deal from him directly during all the summers that I spent with him.

My father was born in California in December of 1934, just after the Great Depression, the eldest of three sons. His father was an attorney and his mother a housewife. Both were alcoholics, which didn't make my father's childhood easy. My dad was in a serious car accident when he was 12, thrown head first through the windshield of a truck. He walked away with over 54 stitches in his face. I feel that may have been the moment that set my dad up with the strength he has had to have throughout his life, and which he taught me.

When my dad turned 17, he enlisted in the Army, which was his one-way ticket out of hell, so he took it.

Let me give you some more history on my father, after all he had lived 48 years before I was even born.

My dad served our country in the United States Army, and was stationed in Ulm, Germany. He climbed up the ranks, and before he was done serving this great country, he was considered an active sergeant.

During his time in the Army, instead of going to the bars and drinking his nights away, he would walk around the streets of Ulm. One day he wandered into a photography art show. This is where he fell in love with photography, which grew into an intense passion.

Dad bought his first camera, an Exakta 35mm, and experimented with photographing anything that was eye-catching. His love for photography blossomed. He returned to the States and attended art school on the GI Bill, which in 1956 gave him a whopping $120 a month to attend school. He went for four semesters and got tired of, as he puts it, "the bullshit."

He then opened his first photography studio, where he lived in the back room. To attract business and clients he would hang photographs of his work taken from Germany to the United States. In those photos I have seen more girls than I can count!

Dad had his studio for a little over a year and then closed it to accept a position as an assistant photographer for Honeywell, where he again moved up the ranks. After he turned down a promotion and a move to Boston, he found himself without a job.

He photographed a roadster (aka: hotrod), which he sold to a magazine for $60! Then he continued to work for that magazine as a freelancer. A man by the name of Jack MacFarland who worked for the *Dodge News Viewer* contacted my father and asked him to take pictures of a muffler; yes, a muffler. My father laughed as he thought it was a joke, but it wasn't. He accepted the job to take pictures of this muffler. He made $27.50, which led to Chrysler contacting him for another job and another, and he worked as a freelancer for Chrysler for more than 20 years.

While he worked for Chrysler, he maintained his freelancing for the magazines and created his own photography business where he photographed new cars, press kits, actors, models, weddings, etc. His business thrived for over 50 years as Chan Bush Photography. He has also contributed photographs and co-authored books and publications.

My dad is well-known when it comes to photography, and has photographed many famous people including Arnold Palmer, Gerald Ford, Bob Hope, Ernie Barnes, Joseph Cotten, Sylvester Stallone, Sally Struthers, Jacques Cousteau, Linda Dano, Kirk Douglas, Parnelli Jones, Magic Johnson, Lawrence Welk, and many, many others. With all of that, I considered my father famous!

I love looking at the black and white photographs my father took, and ones of him as well, which I admire with deep fascination. Every time I look at them my imagination wonders what the true stories are that lie in between the different shades of black and white. My father is an amazingly handsome man and was dubbed *Charming Chan.* Yes, eye roll, but it makes him smile.

He lived so much life before I was even a thought. I have heard so many stories growing up about my dad. Because he was 48 when I was born, most of his extended family had passed. So, to fact check, I relied on his friends, my siblings, and most of all him, the great Charming Chan.

I love listening to him tell stories, but most importantly I love the memories we have made as a father and daughter duo.

My dad believes in tough love, doesn't show affection, and teases you to show that he cares. His favorite word of endearment for me is *dork*. I used to laugh about it and now I roll my eyes and usually follow it with an "Oh, whatever, Dad."

As a kid he would take me golfing, on fun adventures, and sometimes we would go out to eat and sit in silence. As a little girl who loved to talk (except in school) when given the chance, I never understood it and sometimes it drove me crazy.

As you can imagine, sitting in silence was hard and it seemed to last forever. Dad hates noise and loves to be deep in thought. I learned slowly that silence taught me strength, which would be needed in my darkest hours. Strength — physically, mentally, and most importantly, emotionally.

As I got older, I became brave enough to ask him questions. I would ask him what he thought about something or about his life. To me, my dad seemed simple yet mysterious. I was always cautious, but if I asked him something he didn't want to talk about, he would reply with a simple, "I forgot." That was my sign to change the topic.

I didn't know it then, but it was strength that my dad would teach me. I have had many moments that I consider my darkest and those moments I would need to sit in silence. It was in those moments I strengthened myself, my mind, and my desires for life, regardless of all the noise that surrounded me.

My dad taught me that the power of strength is through silence. In those moments you find your strength and you grab hold of it.

Being a child who was bullied, teased, ignored, and ultimately silenced by her peers, I created my own world within the confines of my mind. A world that I could make my own, a world that no others were invited into because it became my castle that was built in silence and housed my strength! A world where no one could hurt me.

It became quite clear that the easiest way to survive a school day and avoid pain was to become an observer of people from the tower within my castle. I learned to take an intentional step back, not to rush, and to slowly disappear in the background, observing in silence the chaos around me.

Learning purposefully how others behaved and taking it in. It took a lot of strength to sit back and be by myself. There were many times I tried to be courageous, to engage with the other kids to see if I would be accepted, only to find I was defeated once again. I wasn't wanted. I was rejected time and time again. I would then again find comfort in my silence, and quickly retreat. I began to see that my strength had a spectrum that wasn't simply black and white. There was a lot of grey area.

As a child, I never did anything unless I was absolutely sure. So, to try again and again to make new friends knowing there was a good chance I would fail took incredible bravery.

We've all heard it: the definition of insanity is doing something over and over again and expecting a different result. Well, that was me. I was not going to give up. I had found a desire to see if life could be different for me. To see if kids could be kind and accepting of me. Every day I failed, yet I tried again the next day.

It didn't stop me. Each time that was unsuccessful, more painful than the last rejection, I became stronger, which only prepared me for the journey ahead.

The strength my dad taught me was ingrained through the observations of my summers and reinforced in the moments of my own solitude. A strength that I could find in my darkest hours when I got knocked down over and over again. A strength that most would define as insane.

My biggest hope is that I never lose sight of the strength I have when silence surrounds me, because it is there I find solace.

To this day, if I feel lost, I sit quietly, allowing my mind to wander, and ultimately finding my strength recharged to conquer any mountain that lies in my path.

Dad, I am very grateful for all the moments we sat in silence, whether it was sharing a meal, playing golf, or the times I was brought along in your Dodge Dart to another job or errand.

I love you, Daddy.

LESSON OF FAITH

My Mrs. Haney

As my summers came to an end, there was one person I always looked forward to seeing as the school year began. Mrs. Haney was my second grade teacher and embraced me from the moment I met her. She taught me a special lesson I hold dear to my heart; she taught me faith.

She was my first friend, mentor, and confidant.

Looking back on the little notes she wrote brings me joy. Back in my day, our grade cards were actual cards and grades were written in pen on paper. Imagine that.

I cherish the comments Mrs. Haney wrote on my grade cards.

First Quarter

> Erin is an excellent student. She is strong in all areas of school. Her phonics grade is lower due to a couple of low test grades, but daily work is tops! I think she gets nervous when a test comes around.
>
> She is a natural leader. She does very well working on group projects in class. Handwriting is lovely, lovely!

Second Quarter

Erin's study habits have improved and she displays more confidence. Her phonics grade went way up as she's worked so hard on it. The grades that went down are all due to a few missed on tests, but like last quarter, daily work is excellent.

Third Quarter

Erin had an excellent quarter! She has really developed excellent study habits which have pulled her through "tough" subjects as skills get more challenging. She is so determined to do well that she never gives up! You couldn't have a better quality!!

She is precious and I'm going to be looking forward to seeing great things happen to her as she continues in elementary school.

Fourth Quarter

Have a great summer! I wanted to have Erin in my room the first day I met her. She brought me much love and happiness. I hope I did the same for her. Much love, Mrs. Haney

In some way, I feel these notes echoed in my soul throughout my life. Since meeting her, her words somehow always kept me going. She has always been the one I wanted to be proud of me. The one that I never wanted to let down. Her words were always genuine and true. She has taught me so much about being a friend, a cheerleader, a supporter, and how to have faith.

I wasn't raised in a religious or spiritual household. When Mrs. Haney came into my life, her kindness resonated with me so much. I can't tell you exactly when her lesson of faith began for me. I can only explain that her believing in me was how I was introduced to the concept of faith. I was lost and she found me, came alongside me, and guided me in my early years. Eventually she taught me about faith in God and unconditional love. However, the concept of unconditional love wouldn't really sink in until much later, when I met my husband.

She always had time for me and embraced me as one of her own. Any time I got bullied she was there to make me feel better. (I was bullied all the way through high school.)

Just knowing I could talk to her about what I was dealing with or that I could sit at her lunch table was what helped me get through the day. Mrs. Haney would teach with an assistant, and not just any assistant, Astro. Astro was a puppet. With his help, I fell in love with learning. He allowed me to have an imagination.

In sixth grade, I had to get braces and Mrs. Haney spoiled me with my favorite foods: a chocolate milkshake, mac n' cheese, and chocolate pudding. That was a great day and a day when all the kids wanted to sit by me at lunch. Keep in mind that before and after this day, the kids wanted nothing to do with me. At lunch, I would get up the courage and try to see if I could be accepted.

I would pick a table and sit down. The moment I sat down, they all picked up their sack lunches or lunch trays and moved immediately away from me. I stayed seated with my head hung down, eating my lunch that was showered with salted tears. It hurt more times than I can count, but I kept trying. Enough was enough, so Mrs. Haney and the rest of the teachers would just have me join them at lunch.

That day, when I was treated with my favorite foods and the kids wanted to be my friends, I ignored them. I realized I didn't want fake friends, friends who only gave me the time of day when they wanted something from me.

I learned on that day that it's better to sit alone than to be surrounded by phony friends. From that moment forward, I learned to accept that if people didn't want to be my friend, I didn't need them as one. Mrs. Haney taught me a lot about morals and values and how it ties to your faith.

She would go to my gymnastic meets and take me to church. Her being there showed me what it meant to have a friend and that friends are there when you need them, no matter what. My family moved around a lot after the seventh grade, but Mrs. Haney and I stayed in touch and I always found my way back to her.

I attended Holt/Kearney schools In Missouri until the eighth grade. My eighth grade year I attended two more schools, one in northern Missouri and the other in California. In high school I attended four different schools:

9th grade: Crescenta Valley HS – California
10th grade: Princeton HS – Missouri
11th grade: Lely HS - Florida
12th grade: Kearney HS - Missouri

Fast forward six years to my senior year at Kearney High School. Like all the years before at previous schools I attended, I went out for golf; I quickly showed my ability on the golf course along with my ambitious personality.

I established my spot on the team as number one and was soon featured in the local paper, *The Kearney Courier*, throughout the season. The golf season was in the fall, and as quickly as the leaves fell from the trees the season was wrapping up.

There was just one more thing to do — qualify for the State Tournament. Both Mrs. Haney and I knew this was my ticket to college. I needed to attend the District Tournament and rank high on the scoreboard to claim my spot at state. Districts that year just happened to fall on my 18th birthday. It was a wet, snowy, and freezing day, but it didn't matter. I had a goal and nothing was going to get in my way.

I had been working towards this my entire life, regardless of doing it alone. My father just happened to be in town for my birthday and he decided that he would attend the golf event, the only golf event he has ever attended to watch me play. Talk about nerves!

Though I was nervous, you wouldn't have known it. I was focused and ready to play regardless of who was watching and how much snow was falling.

It was a long, slow, and freezing round. As the round progressed, I kept my head in the game and warmed up between shots. As I approached the last hole, I knew this could make me or break me. The lesson of strength my dad taught me came into play.

I don't remember the exact score I shot that day, but as we all huddled up on the patio of the golf club and waited for the scores to be finalized and awards to be announced, I waited patiently. It was my birthday, and just having the opportunity that I had to play at Districts for a shot to claim a spot for State had already made my 18th birthday the best.

As I stood there freezing but with excited anticipation, I knew I had played my best. They announced my name, and I placed seventh, qualifying for state! I was ecstatic! Best birthday ever! That meant golf wasn't over and I had work to do.

Now, how does this all link to Mrs. Haney? Well, once I qualified for State, she and her husband Ed insisted I stay with them the night before the big State Tournament! I politely accepted and they made sure I had a healthy and hearty dinner, followed with a good night's sleep and an early morning breakfast.

They saw me off as I drove to the State Tournament in my little red Nissan Sentra. I will never forget the look on their faces as they hugged me goodbye and told me good luck. They stood there embraced in each other's arms, waving to me as I backed out of the driveway.

The State Tournament was like nothing I had ever seen before, but I was overjoyed. The weather was horrible when I arrived, but that wasn't what made me nervous. My mom was actually going to be there to watch me play at State.

This was the first time she had ever shown an interest in my golf and she was going to actually attend an event — not just any event, The Event! I told her the rules and I took my place on the tee box. The bad weather was picking up and it started to rain, but thankfully no lightning so we could play.

Back then we were not as technologically advanced as today's golfers, so when it was wet, so were your hands and glove, which made it quite difficult to grip the club. The hole I teed off on was a short hole; I decided to play it safe and grabbed my 5-iron.

I lined up my shot, took my practice swing behind the ball – literally, not like most golfers, but actually facing the hole — and then stepped up behind my ball and swung as I visualized the shot down the fairway. With intention, I addressed my ball, made a beautiful swing, with perfect impact, and the ball went straight down the fairway. As I followed through, my 5-iron was up in a tree before I knew it.

Yup, that's right. Both my hands and the grip of my club were so wet that it flew right out of my hands and into a tree about 20 feet up. We had five minutes to retrieve the club from the tree or I would be without my 5-iron for the remainder of the round.

I started praying as an official and the girls in my group tried to figure out how we were going to get down my club that was stuck in a pine tree 20 feet up. Mrs. Haney had taught me all about faith. Standing there, looking up into the tree and trying to get my club out of it, I called on my faith and I prayed. Oh, did I pray.

You see, the 5-iron was one of my favorite clubs. Just as our five minutes were almost up, the club fell out of the tree. That right there was pure faith. I know it sounds silly, but amen!

I accomplished so much in my senior year in high school in golf because Mrs. Haney and Ed had so much faith in my ability, and they taught me that I needed to also have faith in myself.

Mrs. Haney is an exceptional human being. She is like no other person I have ever met. She always told me that I was something special and that God had a plan for me. As I write more of my story, I don't know if I completely understand my purpose, but through my experiences I have to think I am getting closer to it.

She introduced me to God and the faith I have in our Heavenly Father. I will be the first to admit, I have loved Him, blamed Him, hated Him and left Him in more ways than I can count. The one thing Mrs. Haney taught me was that regardless of how I was feeling towards God, He would always be there, His love would not falter, and I could count on Him whenever I needed to.

You see, to me Mrs. Haney lives as God intended. She is always there, her love is strong, and I can count on her whenever I need her.

Mrs. Haney is very well-known in the Kearney community, as she has touched so many lives that my story isn't anything special, but she is in *my* story and to me that makes it even more special.

Two of the first people I called when I got my golf scholarship were Mrs. Haney and Ed. They had always supported me in all my endeavors, so it wasn't even a second thought I would call them. She was one of the first to congratulate me on my success and took me out to dinner with her now daughter-in-law to the finest dining in Kansas City. I felt like a princess. It was a night I will never forget. As we celebrated my accomplishments, we were rewarded with a 360-degree view of the city, as this restaurant sat on top of a building and rotated. It was amazing!

When it was time to head off to college and move me into my dorm room, Mrs. Haney was the first to offer her help! I couldn't imagine anyone else better to help move me to college and send me on my way into adulthood. She told me to remember to study hard, love myself, and keep my faith, because God has a plan for me. Mrs. Haney always loved my writing, such as the following poem, one of her favorites.

In a Room

November 10, 2001

In a room by a window
The light fades the shadows face
Music plays
Thoughts run
Moments are done
Peace of mind
Is here
And relaxation takes place
But it's not over
For I can look forward to the time
Left that is in front of me
And enjoy it
Because it matters

After I received my Bachelor of Science Degree in Business Administration, I decided to keep up on my education and enrolled in graduate school to expand my knowledge and qualifications. I finished my last semester in graduate school in December of 2007, but wasn't scheduled to walk across the stage until the following spring.

The walk never happened, but I did receive my MBA degree. You see, in the summer of 2007, I had nothing to do as I had taken all the classes that were being offered. A broken blessing, as I decided to take a co-op (paid internship) in Sunriver, Oregon.

I was working as a bookseller at Barnes and Noble along with my co-op as the Assistant to the Head Golf Professional at Sunriver Golf Resort. That experience showed me that there was more to life than just the Midwest and I was capable of so much more. Mrs. Haney and Ed thought the same. While in Sunriver, I met some of the people who would help jump-start my career in golf.

In January of 2008, I was invited to the PGA Merchandise Show in Orlando, Florida. I just had to get myself there. I did, and I had no fear and approached everyone I could. I made some great connections, which led me to accepting a job as Operations Manager for the PGA Section of Colorado.

When I broke the news to Mrs. Haney and Ed, they were ecstatic. Their response was, "Congratulations! Finally!" You're probably wondering why "finally?" Well, in their eyes I needed to get to new territory to survive and they were right! I needed to get out of the Midwest and make my own way.

They asked, "When are we helping you move?" They helped me pack up my vehicle and their truck and we drove to Colorado a week later. Ed called the trip "The saving of Erin."

They saved me from my past crushing my soul. I will forever be grateful. I had many more lessons that happened after my move to Colorado, but that trip to move me was huge for my survival and allowed me to begin spreading my wings so I could one day fly.

But just like a bird learns to fly, so must I, and before I flew, I had to fall many times over.

However, before I get into that, there is one more person I must share with you, my uncle, Mario Casilli, and the lesson of having pride.

LESSON OF PRIDE

Mario Casilli

December 19, 2001

A man I've known for as long as I can remember
A man of pride, dignity, and honor
A man whose laugh thickens the air
Where wonders come after long days of discussion
Over lunch and small sips of iced tea at the green street café
Considerations far from desires that traveled amongst flowers
About curiosity about my well-being
A man who always gave his love without doubt
A man and his priority all amounted to a simple thought of family and friends
The sky could be gray and he'd brighten it in such a way with a simple smile
A man who loved his life and the way it went
He loved all thoughts and things about him
He and my father the best of friends
Couldn't be broken by the strongest of winds
They are so separate but one
Due to his past he only lets his heart float so far
But didn't let joy of ambition and dedication slip past
His passion for photographs showed his story
And what talent it portrayed with his laughs
He took the grain of sand he was given and turned it to a golden star
A man who gave so much asked for nothing

The man who lived with so much and never thought twice
For he was all a man could and can be
A man who always considered me family
A man, my uncle and my one and only Mario
Mario Casilli, I wear a blue dress for you and you only
Tears fill my eyes when I think of how much I've been given
From a man I've known my whole life
Thank you for all that you've done
You will never know how much you mean to me
Remember you will always be my Mario
And I will always be your girl in the blue dress
I love you Mario and I will always look up to you
You are not only my uncle, but another father
Much pride and love
I'll never forget you

Mario was my dad's best friend, a photographer for *Playboy* magazine, an artist, and much more. To me, he was Uncle Mario, and I loved when my father and I would meet him for lunch, whether it was at Ponderosa, Soup Plantation, or my favorite, Green Street Café.

I would just sit there and watch him drink his sweet tea and talk to my dad about life. I was so impressed with my Uncle Mario and dad, with how they carried a conversation in a way that I would pick up on things they wanted me to and then be completely confused about things that I shouldn't hear.

They had their own secret language, it seemed.

Whenever a young, attractive woman would walk by, that's when the teasing between the two would begin.

One beautiful summer day we were having lunch at the Green Street Café, and a woman walked by, wearing a blue dress. I didn't get a glimpse of her, but boy did both their eyes go wide and their eyebrows jump high.

She must have been something. All I know is Mario looked at Dad, Dad looked at Mario and without hesitation, Mario said, "Wait until Erin is the woman walking by a café in a blue dress." I didn't understand it then, but now I do.

Mario was simply saying that I wasn't going to be this little girl for much longer, and one day two old men might be having lunch when I walk by and they might react the same way to me without my knowledge. Now, don't go thinking anything here. Mario was a photographer for *Playboy*, but he considered it art and not pornography. As all little girls do, I began to grow up and with that the jokes between my father and Uncle Mario became clearer as the years passed. However, it was always fun and games with those two.

I didn't know what a Playmate was. I didn't have a clue. I found out very quickly when my dad thought it would be funny to have me go up to Uncle Mario and say, "I want to be a Playmate!" Mario was quick on his feet and replied back, "Take off your clothes." I said, "Nope." And my father and Mario had a good laugh. It was all innocent fun and it makes me laugh to this day.

I am very important to my father and was just as important to Uncle Mario. He was such a proud man, and we would have extensive conversations about exactly that. He was always proud of me and would remind me that above all else, I needed to be proud of myself.

To never do anything that I didn't want to do. If I do it, I better be proud. He taught me that the opposite of pride was shame and regret, and that no one should force those emotions on you, especially yourself. He taught me to always ask myself, *Will I be proud of this?* If the answer was yes, then I had nothing to worry about.

Living life without pride isn't attractive and sure makes it miserable. He was a man who was always so proud of his life. If something didn't make him proud, he didn't do it, because regret could eat you alive. That doesn't sound appetizing, now does it?

It was the summer after my sophomore year in college when I received the dreadful phone call. Mario had passed. I was devastated.

He had always told me that I would blossom into a beautiful young woman and if I ever wore a blue dress, that would be the day I was no longer the little girl, but a grown woman who could make both him and my dad proud. It would be the day that Dad would realize his little girl is all grown up. I never got to wear a blue dress for Mario.

I cried. I cried because I didn't get to say goodbye, and I felt betrayed that no one told me how close he was to dying so I could talk with him one more time and say my goodbyes.

I mean, after all, I had seen him just several months earlier during the holiday break my freshman year in college, and everything seemed like he was getting better. Below is a journal entry from December 15, 2001, that I wrote after I saw Mario.

> December 15, 2001: I saw Mario Casilli yesterday. My uncle. No one told me what was going on until a few days ago. No matter what he will always be my Mario and I will always love him. It hurts to think how much pain he's in. I know he knows that I love him. I don't want to cry, but I need to, and to tell you the truth, I will

tonight before I go to bed. I just want to sit with him for a while by myself and talk and share my poem. Let him know how much he means to me and tell him I love him.

I know it won't be goodbye, yet I want him to know he's the best. He has taught me much that I have yet to know of. I miss him so much. He is still my Mario. The thing I don't understand is that only seven months ago he wasn't in great health, but he seemed as if he was getting better. I just feel that I have so much to tell him. Well, I need to go to bed. Good night. EB

I realized after he passed that he still saw me as that little girl who needed to be sheltered. That was a moment I will never forget: when I realized he wouldn't see me grow up, hear my poems, see me marry or one day have kids.

I loved my Mario; he was family and he taught me that you must always have pride for the life you're living. And if you don't, you had better rethink and change the direction you're going.

It gives me hope to think that wherever my Mario is, I am not only making myself proud but making him proud of the way I am living my life. So, if you ever see me wearing a blue dress, just know it's a shout out to him and a statement of the pride I have for the life I live.

ERIN BAER

LESSON OF LOYALTY AND FRIENDSHIP

Jennifer – Bestie

At Rosemont Junior High in California, my third eighth grade school that year, I was determined to make a fresh start. No bad memories to follow me.

Dad got me signed up for eighth grade and dropped me off the first day so he could show me the route I would have walk to school. It was uphill, over the highway, and more than a mile away.

How exciting — an outside campus so we could enjoy the sunlight every day! Well, this was the year of El Niño. Even though we got our sunny days, we also got our rainy days.

The worst part wasn't having to walk to school, but the fact that El Niño meant a downpour of rain. With no good drainage system, I was walking sometimes in a foot of water, and by the time I arrived to school I was soaked. But it didn't matter because our campus and classrooms also flooded. Luckily, it didn't rain every day.

It was lunch time on a sunny day during my first week of school. With courage on my side, I strutted into the quad at the top of the amphitheater. I saw the one person I knew, a family friend, Jennifer B. I said hello, and she quickly introduced me to a few other people.

One girl she introduced me to quickly became my lifelong best friend, Jennifer L. We hit it off right away. Finally, a friend! I hadn't ever known what that felt like, but I was ecstatic.

Here I was — new state, new school, and a friend! I couldn't believe it. How exciting!

She was short, blonde, athletic, and beautiful. She was popular too. *How cool,* I thought. *A popular girl who wants to be my friend.*

After that day, we spent every lunch together and really nurtured our friendship. I loved having a friend, and her mom was awesome. On some of those rainy days I had to walk to school, they would pick me up from my house or they would go the route I walked just in case they could catch me and give me a ride. It was awesome and felt great that other people actually cared about me — not only that, but they wanted to hang out with me, too!

We had the best time and our friendship blossomed quickly. She played soccer and we would hang out when she didn't have soccer practice. Her practices were intense. Unfortunately, she injured herself and needed ACL surgery. I felt so bad for her. She was going to be out for a while and wouldn't be able to resume soccer until months later.

While she was out for knee surgery, she missed out on a scary and traumatic event that took place at our junior high school. The week after her surgery, while she was recovering at home, I walked to school as I normally did, but it was anything but a normal day. I arrived at my school and saw police cars surrounding the area, police officers and SWAT everywhere. I was confused, scared, and knew something was not right. I was greeted just as all the other students were by a person of importance at the school. We were told to make our way to the lower field, find our first period teacher and to stay there until further notice. We were not allowed to walk around campus, go to our lockers or any other area. Good thing the weather wasn't too bad. The walk down to the lower field was awful, as I had just limped over a mile to get to school on an ankle I had sprained a few days before, and now I had to do more walking. *Are you kidding me?*

When I arrived, we were informed that a bomb had been found on one of our classroom doors, but not to panic. *Ugh, I'm sorry, what?* However, it wasn't just a random door, it was my math teacher whose door had the bomb fixed to it. As the minutes and hours passed, students and teachers were questioned, and an investigation was underway while the SWAT team led a mission to disarm the bomb.

Towards the end of our four-hour stint doing nothing except playing silly games and remaining cooperative, while the disarming of the bomb took place on the softball/baseball fields, we were all warned there would be a large explosion, but they assured us that our safety came first.

There was indeed a large explosion. Luckily the bomb was carefully removed from the targeted teacher's door, taken by a robot to the fields and destroyed. Talk about surreal. Here I was, 14 years old and dealing with a bomb threat that in fact was a real bomb at my school. *Say what?* And I didn't have my best friend, since she was home recovering from surgery.

Once the officials and SWAT team confirmed the clearance of the device and that the rest of the school property was clear, we were told to go to the front of the school, where parents were waiting for their kids. Those of us who were walkers were also finally free to go home. School resumed the next day.

Going to school the next day was strange, especially math class. We could see where the bomb had been on the doorknob and rumors began to surface about why someone would target our teacher.

The strangest part is that the suspect was the boy who sat in front of me in math class and was also my assigned gym partner. It was an eerie feeling. I just thought he was weird and liked to stay to himself. *How could something so dangerous be thought up by someone I went to school with, let alone an eighth grader?* He was suspended and not allowed to come back for the remainder of the year.

I am just thankful my friend Jennifer didn't have to go through the trauma of that day. Not because she would have gotten hurt, but because of knowing that a classmate wanted to hurt a person intentionally, and possibly blow up the school. That is not something you just get over.

I actually just recently asked her if she remembers the bomb and she can't recall it, but her parents do and they are also thankful she wasn't at school that day.

At the beginning of the summer, we would hang out and go to the beach, or hang out at Verdugo Hills Golf Course. We had a great time. Then I went back to Missouri to visit my mom and sister. It was miserable; I couldn't wait to go back to California. During my summer visit I was put to work; I had to do all the chores, clean the kitchen, the bathrooms, do the laundry, sweep the floors, vacuum, take out the trash, and take care of the dogs. Sure, it taught me great skills, but my sister didn't have to do any of it and just hung out with all of her friends. So, when it was time to go back to California, you bet I had a grin on my face.

When I came back, Jennifer and I picked up right where we left off. Our first year in high school was about to start. We decided to get a locker together so we could always have each other's back. Ninth grade started off fantastic! I loved my classes; I had a friend who was introducing me to so many more people and I was making friends!

My dad always loved celebrating my birthday and he was sneaky for my 15th. He was able to get my brothers, their significant others, and himself to throw me a surprise birthday party. I walked into the house, and surprise! They were all there. I was bummed though — I had really wanted my best friend to be there and she was nowhere to be found. I even asked Dad if she was coming and he told me that she had prior obligations and couldn't make it. I was slightly disappointed, but I understood. After all, her soccer schedule was insane. Dad told me to go get something, and when I turned the corner in the small one-bedroom apartment that I shared with my dad I ran right into her. It was the best surprise ever! She came to celebrate my 15th birthday.

Dad had done a golf theme for the party, of course. After all, what else would it be? Jennifer and I had so much fun that day, along with my family. She was so thoughtful and got me a golf-themed necklace. I wore that necklace every day. I had a best friend, and I was on the boys' golf team, what could be better than that?

The first half of ninth grade was fantastic. I felt on top of the world and I didn't think anything could destroy my new-found life and my friendship with Jennifer.

A few weeks before the end of the school year, we had a misunderstanding and our friendship fell apart. At the end of the year, I had nothing. I felt that since no one liked me here and no one liked me in Missouri, and since living with Dad in a one-bedroom apartment was tough, I should go back to Missouri. My twin sister always talked about how she missed me and how much independence she had, so I thought it would be better to go back where maybe I could be liked if I gave it another shot.

When I told Jennifer I was moving, she begged me to stay, but I told her no. *Why would I stay?* I told her I didn't want to be somewhere I wasn't wanted. She didn't understand that if Missouri was bad and now California was bad, why wouldn't I stay? She tried to convince me to stay again and I told her that I had already made my decision and I was leaving after school was out for the summer. I told her that maybe I could start all over again, in Missouri. Maybe it would be different. I soon discovered that I couldn't have been more wrong.

When I went back to Missouri, it was just like the previous summer when I visited. I did all the chores, had to also find a job, and any dime I made was turned over to my mom. Here I was at 15, supporting the family in more ways than one. A real-life Cinderella without the Prince Charming. As soon as I was 16, I became the chauffeur for my twin sister. If she needed a ride or grocery shopping needed to be done, it was up to me. How miserable. Not only did I miss my friend Jennifer, I didn't have any friends in Missouri as they were all my sister's. She had established territory and I was not wanted. The only good thing was that I took the number one spot on the women's golf team and was admired by coaches from the different schools in the nearby towns for my incredible golf skills. I *felt* like a small-town celebrity, but that too came with consequences of not being liked by my peers. I didn't have an ego, I just wanted others to be proud of me; that's all I ever wanted.

The summer finally came and I had to work, but I did get to take a trip to California to visit my dad, with hopes I could make amends with Jennifer. I thought maybe enough time had passed that she would forgive me and would want to be friends with me. Back then we didn't have cell phones. We had the phones that were tied to walls, and you had to wait for a dial tone and push real buttons to make a call. Once I was in California and a few days passed, I got up the courage to make the call. The phone rang and her mother picked up the phone. I asked for Jennifer, and lo and behold, she took my call. Wow. Before she could say anything, I said my name and asked if she could just listen. She did.

I went on to explain that I missed her, she was my best friend and I hoped we could be friends again. I was shocked when she told me that she was sorry for accusing me of stealing her yearbook, that she actually found it in this other friend's backpack, and that she missed me too. She asked if I could ever forgive her, and of course I did.

Since I moved away after my freshman year of high school, we have always lived far apart, but we haven't missed a beat in our relationship since.

Most recently, I went to visit her in November 2018 before I was scheduled for surgery. I drove the nine hours to a small town on the west side of Wyoming, up in the mountains, to be welcomed by my best friend, her husband, and their three adorable boys. We spent the weekend hiking in the snow, catching up, and playing airplane with the boys. It was such a wonderful trip that forced me to get off the grid, out of my own head, and enjoy nature and all the beauty that surrounds us, even when I found myself in a valley of life.

We both have pretty busy schedules, her running a household and running after three boys; me, running several businesses and working on having a family of my own. But we manage to always find time to catch up or send a video message when time freezes even for a minute.

Jennifer is a true friend, one who has taught me the importance of friendship, loyalty and what forgiveness is all about. Even though we had a break in our relationship as very young and naïve teenagers, we were able to pick up where we left off once we mended our broken relationship.

I never stopped considering myself a friend to her because I just knew we would find our way back to each other, whether it was in the next year or even several years later. Thank God it was the following summer.

She taught me that regardless of the decisions others make, you can remain loyal as long as you know it is for the right reasons. Your word goes far beyond the mistakes that can happen, and as long as you are truthful and your actions match up, then anything can be mended.

We have been friends for over 21 years and both know that our friendship has and always will be true and loyal, regardless of what stages we are at in life. We can always lean on one another, talk things out, love one another, have our differences, and still remain supportive of each other. Time will pass, but our friendship will never die.

Jennifer and I have never doubted our commitment to our relationship since we reconnected all those summers ago. That is true friendship and loyalty. We have never taken each other for granted and I don't think we ever will. I love her as my sister and I look up to her more than she may ever know.

Chapter 2

Golf as the Rock – Consistency

Sacrifice glory for failure, so when success comes you will understand the blessing behind life. –Erin Baer

Golf is my love. I was fortunate to find my love for golf at a very young age, which my father is responsible for. Not only did he teach me the lesson of strength, which comes in very handy in the game of golf, he taught me the game that I would find comfort in and learn to develop a lifelong relationship with. To me, golf is not just a sport, but a relationship I participate in. I know it sounds strange but it will make sense as you read on.

The legend is that my dad taught me to golf when I was two. My mom said that we'd go to the golf course, Dad would have me put the ball on the tee and he would hit it. She thought he was going to hit my head but he never did. Then it went to putting. He never bought me kids' plastic clubs; he cut down a regular Blade Northwestern putter. I played with that until I was 15 years old, literally bent over. (Even though I have never been that tall). Every summer that I stayed with him we would spend all our days at the golf course. We'd be at the putting green or at the range or in the pro shop or playing the Loop, which was four holes that looped out from the clubhouse and back in. It was a par-three course, so it was a small course.

Golf was where I could just be myself. It was something I was actually good at. I never really had to take a lesson. I was always learning how to get better at golf, and had golf mentors who wanted to see me swing and hit the ball, because I had and still do have such a beautiful swing. I just have a natural ability.

Luckily, these mentors have embraced me in my search for the perfect score in golf. While growing up, I thought they were giving me lessons in golf, when in fact they were giving me lessons in life.

My mentors are amazing. Though some of them have passed and some are now very old, they left their mark on me as a golf ball leaves its mark on a putting green.

Golf has always been my rock of consistency; a way I could relate to life where otherwise I was confused.

Even if golf is a lone sport, I felt that I had a belonging amongst others.

I loved keeping score. Regardless if it was a good score, a great score, or a horrible score, I held onto those scorecards. I not only filled them out with my name, the date, my scores for each hole, but if you look closely at the scorecards, starting in 1997 you will find a comment written by me to myself on each one.

I became my own cheerleader in the sport; I congratulated myself, I disciplined myself, I gave myself advice, and I learned from myself.

I kept a collection of all my scorecards from my summers as a reminder that I always found a little piece of heaven on earth and it was where I fit in, where I could be true to myself, and regardless of the score, I was somebody.

Date: March 15, 1997
Golf Course: Avila Golf (Par: 62)
Playing with: Dad
Score: 78
Front nine: 50
Comment: *Improving. Keep it up!*

Date: April 16, 1997
Golf Course: Verdugo Hills Golf Course
(Par-3 course: 27)
Playing with: Cindy, Katie, Jerry
Score: 37 (back nine only)
*Note: I had two birdies that day
Comment: *Good Job!*

Date: April 20, 1997
Golf Course: Verdugo Hills Golf Course
(Par-3 course: 27)
Playing with: Russ
Score: 35 (back nine only)
Comment: *Best Score so far! Keep Working.*

Date: April 23, 1997
Golf Course: Verdugo Hills Golf Course
(Par-3 course: 27)
Playing with: myself
Score: Didn't keep score, but took note that I got a BIRDIE on the Hardest Hole #16
Comment: *Good Job!*

Date: April 27, 1997
Golf Course: Verdugo Hills Golf Course
(Par-3 course: 27)
Playing with: myself
Score: 42 (back nine only)
Comment: + *You worked hard all day, don't worry about it! (Seven buckets)*

LESSON OF PASSION AND TENACITY

What My Big Brother Taught Me

When I lived in California, I started playing golf with my half-brother Tyler (my dad's son). I started seeing my score dropping and my game improving. My hard work was finally paying off. Slowly but surely, I was finally *underpar* at Verdugo! Over the course of that year I began beating my brother Tyler more often than not. He's my big brother and he likes to make comments that I was just lucky or he let me win. However, it's just his way of being my big brother and giving me a hard time, but also letting me know I had skill and to keep at it. It was such an amazing time that I will always cherish with my older brother Ty. I have always admired him, as he taught me a valuable lesson of always dreaming big and never stopping.

Tyler and I have always been close. We look very much alike and are both left-handed. So we got one another; being lefties was our thing. I would spend many summer days with him in the garage at his mom's house, where he lived, slept, ate, wrote, sang and recorded music. It was fascinating. I was so impressed with the passion and tenacity he had for his art/talent. I was in love with the love he had for what he truly enjoyed. It inspired me.

I took what I learned from watching him make his music and applied it to my love for golf. Golf was mine like music was Ty's. I still admire my big brother.

We are only 14 years apart, but when I was just a child, I thought he was so mature and sophisticated. Yet, he was just a young adult pursuing his dreams. I held onto that. *If he could do it, then so could I.* After all, it must be the power of being in the right mind (being left-handed — it's an expression ... LOL). My brother and I have a respect for one another that doesn't need to be spoken. We are proud of one another and truly do love each other unconditionally. We have never argued and we have always loved each other as it was always intended for a brother and sister. We don't compete or compare; we're each other's cheerleader and support.

Over time, my confidence grew and I fell in love with the game over and over again. It kept me grounded and focused. It gave me something that I could turn to during my hardest times as well as my happiest times. It was always there; I could rely on it. Even if I took a break, I always knew I could come back and it would still be able to make me happy.

LESSON OF PATIENCE AND PERCEPTION

Dan and Rose

As a child, patience was not something I had. I was all about the present. For me, I wanted to know all the whys and hows, so being patient wasn't really an option. However, learning golf at such a young age, patience was an inevitable quality you needed to learn and possess.

Every summer growing up I would visit my dad in sunny Southern California. Most probably would assume California was my escape, and it was, but not in the way you would think. Going to California was a way for me to be my authentic self. Growing up in the shadows of my twin sister and my little sister was difficult, especially since in my mom's household golf was frowned upon and not considered a real sport. My twin sister was a phenomenal runner. In fact, she was so amazing she made the front page of *The Kansas City Star*.

My little sister was a blossoming soccer player. Because those two sports were friendlier to the spectator, I, along with my love of golf, was forgotten about and pushed to the back burner.

So, as always, I did my thing as a party of one. I took my stance, kept my head down, and took my shots. I perfected this over days, weeks, months and even years of practice, not only in golf but in my life as well. My earlier years were quite lonely. Therefore,

California was exciting to me. And every summer I always looked forward to going to California, hanging out at Verdugo Hills Golf Course with my friends and mentors and playing golf.

All my friends were much older, so much older in fact they were my parents' and grandparents' ages. I didn't care; to me age was just a number. I have always felt I had an old soul, so being with my older friends and mentors, I felt most at home, especially on the golf course.

Dan and Rose were the most beautiful and classy couple I had ever met. I was lucky enough to call them my friends, and Dan was one of my first golf mentors. They remind me of the old black and white films and the love stories the movies would tell. So undeniably in love with each other and very respectful of the time they had together.

I'm not quite sure how old I was when I first met Dan and Rose, but the memories of them both, and our times together, have been with me for as long as I can remember.

Dan and Rose would always sit at the green picnic table by the back of the pro shop, under a great big tree that shaded the patio area.

Dan was a wise man with a shaved head who sat quietly with his arms crossed, observing the golfers and the world around him while living in deep thought.

He always wore a nice pair of clean pressed pants and a bright, collared shirt; usually it was blue to match his blue eyes. Rose would wear a long-sleeved blouse, gloves, a beautifully hand-knitted hat, and sunglasses to shade her from the sun. She was very sensitive to the sun and she always took the necessary precautions to protect herself, but did so with beauty.

Any time my dad and I would go to Verdugo, I would run in and through the pro shop to the gathering area where I would hope to see Dan and Rose and all my buddies, because I knew I would be greeted with hellos, hugs, and "How are you?"

As energetic as I was, Dan and Rose would always have a way to capture me in the moment and mesmerize me with stories and lessons. Dan enjoyed watching me hit the ball and encouraged me to go to the range for a lesson. I never passed up the opportunity to get a lesson from him. He always made me feel like a star.

As I warmed up, he would watch, and just at the right time he would give me instruction. But before he ever gave me his professional advice, he encouraged me to think for myself. He would ask me, "What did you do wrong?" Or, "What happened that caused the ball to get off course?" I couldn't ever get away with saying, "I don't know," and he always told me to at least try telling him what I thought the problem was. If I was wrong or didn't think about it, he would just tell me to think harder.

He would first ask me, "Where did the ball go, why did it go that way, and how do you fix it?"

At first, I would get frustrated that he wouldn't just tell me. However, having me think about my shot backwards from result to cause would not only teach me patience, but perception — how to look at things.

It was an amazing way to teach, which ultimately, I adopted as my way of teaching.

If you only look at things one way, you limit your ability to overcome obstacles and problems with different solutions. There isn't just one way of doing things, but a multitude of ways. I always encourage my golfing students to think for themselves, because they already know the answer and the solution. When they get stuck, I do what Dan always did. I walk through the shot with them so they understand their swing better and can then self-correct when they are on their own. Dan taught me so much about how to be patient with myself when it came to golf and my game, that it has stuck with me my entire life. I am very capable of analyzing my swing on the course and correcting it appropriately to move on to the next shot, without getting hung up on the last. This ultimately seeped over into my life. If you only look at things one way, you miss so much. As in golf, so it is in life and business. First, you must look at the smaller pieces, and after you do, you must step back and see the bigger picture.

I love the ability to see things from many different perspectives and watching resolutions unfold. I also have taken it one step further to make sure that I keep an open mind to others' perspectives, which allows me to see a much bigger picture.

If it hadn't been for Dan and his ability to be extremely patient with me while showing me that the answers always lie within, then my perception would be very one-dimensional.

I think of Dan and Rose often, and I miss them very much. I know that both Dan and Rose have long passed. Wherever they may be, I hope they can see the impact they had on me from a very young age. They were always smiling while getting me to think for myself. They taught me to think for myself and to look at golf shots (and life) from different views. One view is not enough to come to a conclusion.

LESSON OF CONCENTRATION

Bob Kane

"Enjoy the simple things through great concentration." These may not be the exact words that he spoke to me, but it is the lesson that he left for me. I will never forget Bob Kane.

Every summer at Verdugo Hills Golf Course, my dad would either be practicing his game, chatting it up with the boys, or in the pro shop working.

Any time I showed up I would go search for my buddies (all the Men's Club men) and Bob Kane was always one of my favorites. He was like an uncle to me, always greeting me with that grin of his along with a big bear hug. Bob was a tall man who walked with a limp due to a bad hip. He smoked cigarettes, which I didn't understand since he had a heart problem. He always wore a smile.

Back in those days there was a fence that surrounded the putting green at Verdugo Hills Golf

Course and a turnstile gate to get in. That's where Bob liked to hang out. He would talk to me for hours and always gave me great advice. Bob was so simple in his lessons; he was a man who didn't have to say much to get his point across.

He was very skilled in his ability to concentrate. You could see it in his eyes. Any time we played a game on the putting green or had a little fun competition (even though I didn't realize he was teaching me), he would focus with intensity before each shot. Without hesitation, he would line up, take his stroke and sink his putt. He made it look effortless. I began studying him and trying to copy what he did. I wanted to have an intensity about me when I played the game. I wanted to be aggressive with my putts, leave hesitation behind. *Commit!* He taught me how to become very skilled in concentration. I would ask him, "How did you do that?" which was my way of saying, "Please show me."

He taught me how to read the greens. I learned this from other mentors as well, but he showed me how to focus on a point between the ball and the hole. That is where you put your concentration. Whether from the tee box to the fairway, or the fairway to the green, or the ball to the hole, there was always a spot you needed to concentrate on first, before the destination of the shot. I admired that about him. In fact, I was infatuated. I wanted to learn this ability that seemed like a superpower. He was always willing to play the Loop with me, tell me what a joy it was to watch me swing the club, and given any opportunity he would speak his wisdom over me. I welcomed it. He and I had the same favorite hole at Verdugo: number 13. I still love that hole. I admired Bob Kane so much that I always envisioned getting a hole-in-one on that exact hole, the one that completed the Loop.

Bob was so proud of me and my dedication to the game that in 1998 he organized the greatest surprise when I was going out for the boys' golf team at Crescenta Valley High School. I was so nervous. How intimidating: a freshman female in high school trying out for golf. The school had no women's team, so I tried out for the boys' team. I was so scared, and I didn't want to disappoint anyone, especially my friend Bob.

I showed up to tryouts with my four-club golf set and a bag that had my name on it written in pastel yellow and flowers to match. Talk about embarrassing.

Bob told me, "Just keep your head down, do your best, and that in itself is good enough. Nothing more, nothing less." So I did just that.

Well, tryouts were over and I was about to find out if I made the team or not.

When Bob found out I was trying out for the golf team, and only had a four-club set, he didn't think it was good enough, yet he knew it wouldn't change my determination and focus on doing my best.

Bob got all the Verdugo Men's Club members (my buddies) to donate to a fund he organized to buy me my very first real set of golf clubs! He was successful, and the day I found out I made the team was the same day I told my buddies and received my surprise set of clubs. I did outgrow them, but I still have them. I just can't part with them because they hold a special place in my heart.

After I moved back to Missouri, Bob passed away. I was devastated. A true confidant, friend, and teacher had passed and I didn't understand why. I found out it was due to his heart; it just couldn't fight anymore. On our favorite hole, number 13, they placed a stone "In memory of Bob Kane" at the tee box. Every time since that I've played the course and gotten to that hole, I take a moment of silence, kiss my fingers and place them on the stone and say hi to my friend. I always dedicate that tee shot to him before I step up to the tee box. Whether the shot was good or bad, I knew he was watching. I could feel his presence and how proud he was of me. A few years later, my brother Tyler and I were playing golf at Verdugo Hills, and guess what? I got my very first hole-in-one on that exact hole. I had envisioned what my hole-in-one would look like over and over again. It happened just like I had envisioned all those times before. I knew in that very moment that Bob was right there celebrating in my joy! I miss him more than I can express, but I know that he is one of my angels, and has my back and my swing.

He always used golf as an analogy for life, and he taught me so much through those analogies. In golf, just as in life, if you concentrate hard enough and practice enough, you can master it. I know I have a lot of practice left, and I am not a master by any means, but with enough concentration and will, I can be successful in life.

Any time I lose focus, I just remember Bob Kane and how he told me that making a decision to concentrate is the first step, and after that it gets easier to tackle the task at hand. I will forever be grateful to him, for playing the Loop, showing me how to conquer the art of concentration, and being one of my biggest fans. I miss him dearly.

LESSON OF INTEGRITY

Dick Saatzer

Integrity is a quality I hold dear to not only my heart, but my soul. Integrity means the quality of being honest and having strong moral principles; moral uprightness. If you don't have that, then what do you have? Dick Saatzer is a true man of integrity who helped instill this great quality in me. He was a Golf Pro at Verdugo Hills Golf Course, a friend of my dad's, and another one of my golf mentors. I have been truly lucky to have had these great influences in my life. He taught me so much about integrity, just by being himself. I was lucky enough to record a few of our conversations back in 2015 and I am so glad I did. Sharing the following conversation allows me to explain the lesson of integrity better and shows you in his own words what kind of man he is.

At the course, I was on the range and hitting balls. I wanted Dick to see that I still had it. He did give me a lesson that day, as he always did when he had the chance. I never took any of his lessons for granted, especially those that were life lessons.

That one conversation I had with Dick became a great life lesson. I knew he was getting older. I also had a feeling my visits to California were drawing to a close. Since I always respected him and valued his advice, I never took it for granted. I wanted to know his one piece of advice that would be helpful to me throughout my life.

Me: If you had to give me any advice for the rest of my life, what would it be?

Dick Saatzer: Be yourself. Do what you feel that you have to do. To feel that, you do what you want to do, not what you have to do. Basically, if you are going into a sport that you know, be a good teacher. That's the main thing. Be a good instructor, a good teacher so that everybody can understand what you're doing. The problem with teachers is they don't stay down on the ground floor with their pupils. In golf, it takes two people to make a golf swing. It takes the pupil and the teacher, and if the teacher stays above the pupil then they'll never improve. The teacher has to get down on your level. So, if you are teaching someone muscle building, you have to get right there too. "This is how I want you to do it, now remember, I am going to turn your muscles, so you can feel it and do it." That's the best thing you can do. Be a good teacher. Be yourself. Don't be somebody else. Don't be phony. That's the main ingredient of life is, don't put on a show for people, be, be, be who you are and that's it.

Me: That's good advice!

Dick Saatzer: Well you know, there's too many people out there who are trying to be somebody they're not. If I felt that you couldn't teach your sport, I'd say, "Erin, try something else." You're gonna go through some rough spots, but you know what? Just keep, keep plugging. If you're going to be a teacher, just be a good teacher.

Me: Well, I can do that!

Dick Saatzer: That's right! I know you can! That's why I tell ya. Be what you want to be.

I am so glad I recorded it, because I knew I would want to listen to it over and over again. The words still echo in my heart and mind.

Dick is such an important role model to me, as he always taught me to live a life with integrity – because if you don't have integrity then nothing else matters.

When I am faced with a challenge, I remind myself of this very lesson. The lesson of integrity is not one I take lightly; when my life ends, I want to know that I always lived with the utmost integrity and made my dear friend and mentor Dick proud.

LESSON OF ENCOURAGEMENT AND DETERMINATION

Coach Capra

Over the course of high school, I attended four different schools, in three different states. The only thing I had that gave me peace of mind was golf. I was teased because I was a jock; a girl who played golf. I was called everything from nerd to dyke, loser to stuck up. All because I was female and I played what many considered a man's sport.

The one good thing for me was the pleasure I found in playing golf and excelling at it. I was good. I was number one on my teams from my sophomore to senior year and was constantly talked about in the local papers — I was a star in the golf world back in my day. I wish I would have realized it then, but I cherish all my golf moments.

Erin's High School Golf Summary

Lettered in golf all four years as one of the top golfers

- **Freshman Year**
  - Played on boy's golf team at Crescenta Valley, CA: Pacific League Champions
- **Sophomore Year**
  - Played in Princeton, MS

- **Junior Year**
  - Played at Lely High School in Florida
  - Participated in the Sixth Annual Larry Bird Masters Golf Tournament
- **Senior Year**
  - First Team All-Conference
- **School Records**
  - Team Dual Score: 202
  - Season Team Average: 222.1
  - Dual Individual Score (Broke school record for lowest score after 13 years by three strokes with a 43)
  - Individual Season Average 48.1
  - State Qualifier
  - Placed 34th out of 120 girls (rained out the first day, so only one day to compete)
  - Seven-time Medalist

The final high school I attended was back in Missouri, because my mother disowned me at 17. When she dropped me off to live with my ex-stepdad and half-sister, she told me I was a terrible daughter. She later emailed me to say she no longer wanted anything to do with me.

From that time until I turned 18, I received a portion of her Social Security check every month for living expenses. I was declared independent by the state.

So during my senior year I was playing for Kearney High School, focusing on golf and academics while also working after school. We had a conference tournament and I needed a ruling on a particular hole with a shot that, well, didn't go as planned. The girls in my group had hurried to their shots, and I called out to them to help with this ruling, but no one acknowledged me.

I looked up and in the gallery I saw an older gentleman walking along with our group. I thought he was a parent or spectator of some sort, maybe a coach. I asked him, "What should I do?"

He politely told me that I was to ask the girls in my group, that he couldn't advise me, and I had to make a decision according to the rules.

I was completely lost! I decided to do the ruling I knew. I took my penalty and proceeded with the round. It was the right decision. *Whew, that was close!*

I didn't see this man again until after the state tournament. That season, I had heard about Rockhurst University, but didn't know anything about the school except the things one of the girls on my team had told me. She was hoping to go there to play golf. I was just hoping any school would take me to play golf. I didn't care what school; any would do.

My high school golf coach told me of the possibility of playing golf for Rockhurst University.

Rockhurst then contacted me to set up a meeting to see if they were a good fit for my educational goals, and you guessed it — *golf*!

I was shocked! I had been working my entire life toward this goal and knew that my only shot at going to college was through my skills in golf. It had been a lonely game in both golf and in life up to this point, but it didn't stop me from forging a strong relationship with the game.

The meeting took place at my high school. When I walked in to the room to meet Rockhurst University's golf coach I was pleasantly surprised — he was the man from the tournament! The man I had asked for advice from and who had politely told me he could only observe and not talk to the players. I was stunned, but it all made sense. He was there scouting for the following year, but not just anybody – little 'ole me!

I shook his hand, took a seat, and a conversation about me, my educational goals, and my golf career took place. He explained that day he was there scouting me and was impressed with my game, my attitude, and how I handled myself on the course. He told me how he had been watching me all season and he was there to offer me acceptance into Rockhurst University with a golf scholarship!

I couldn't believe it! My hard work was finally getting the recognition it deserved and was paying off! Wow! When I played golf in California, I was encouraged. But everywhere else I was told it would never happen, that I would never be a good enough golfer to receive a scholarship. However, being told I couldn't do it only fueled me more to show that I could! To prove them wrong! All the naysayers, all the negative words that were spoken to me, all the jokes and mean comments, they didn't matter anymore. I had *finally* proved them wrong! In reality, I was starting to show myself that I was enough.

I always thought that if I did one more thing, I would be enough for others. Ultimately, always accomplishing things that people told me I couldn't do gave them more reasons to reject me. It didn't matter what I accomplished; the haters always hated. They constantly said I wouldn't or I couldn't. It was something that, to me, wouldn't make sense until I was well into my 30s, but as an 18-year old girl, getting a golf scholarship was my biggest win up to that point!

I thought, *Maybe I am good enough.*

Getting the offer of the golf scholarship to Rockhurst University was honestly the first time I felt good enough for something, something I had been chasing after my whole life.

I felt a sense of accomplishment and justification for all the endless practicing and lonely rounds of golf. I was standing on top of the mountain showing everyone what I was capable of.

But it's funny, because when I was in the moment of thinking I was proving them wrong, that's not what it was really about. The point of pursuing a dream consciously, I thought it was about "showing people up." After all, I was constantly being confronted by challenging competitions at home, so why would this be any different? It was. It was about me, myself, and I and showing that, despite the beliefs of others and the negative voice that echoed in my mind – the one that gave room to those thoughts and allowed me to listen to the naysayers – when I got recruited to play golf, something shifted. It showed me a different way of thinking: that I held the power all along to succeed, as long as I believed in myself.

It was hard to believe in myself, however I constantly pushed through. When Coach Cap came into my life, he told me that he believed in me and I should always believe in myself, regardless of any circumstance.

I borrowed his belief in me until my self-belief grew.

Finally, my first semester in college and I was a collegiate athlete preparing to play my little heart out. Practice was every day. We would hit balls, practice putting, and if the course wasn't busy, we would play. I loved golf practice. I was able to play in a couple of tournaments until one day during practice I got severely hurt. It was hole number 10 on our home practice course, and my tee shot went to the right and rolled under a tree. I didn't think anything about it and assessed the shot I needed to take.

I grabbed my 5-iron and decided to do a low bump out shot. Well, I did and as I followed through, to avoid tree branches I over-cocked my left wrist, and, *Snap!* Oh, the pain! It began swelling instantly. I continued to play, but after each shot, I had to let go of the club with my left hand. It was excruciating, but I am stubborn. I finished the round and afterwards decided I should probably go get checked out by our athletic physical therapist. The next day I did, and just like that I was out for the season.

I was completely devastated and disappointed. It was my first season and I was benched.

As much as it sucked to sit out from practice and tournaments, I didn't let it get me down. Though I was injured, I still attended every practice, encouraging my teammates and showing my support on game days. After all, I was still part of the team; I just had a different role now. Coach taught me that just because things don't go as planned doesn't mean it's over. He taught me that it was the perfect time to prepare myself for what's to come. He encouraged me to do what I could for my mindset and to stay determined to get stronger. Be present, complete my sports therapy, and encourage the team by showing up and letting them know how strong we are as a team even when one member is unable to play due to uncontrollable circumstances. He taught me that encouraging others would only come back as encouragement for myself and keep me determined to fight for my gift.

His encouragement showed me to look beyond myself and look to my teammates to help keep me focused, by giving them the support they needed.

Attending practice, even though I wasn't required to, gave me the determination to push myself both mentally and physically so I could be back to 100 percent for the following season.

There were days that I struggled, days when I thought it wouldn't matter to my teammates if I didn't show up or missed practice. Other days I thought they wouldn't even notice. Yet those were the days I promised to show up because it wasn't about me, it was about my team. I didn't want to let them down. Those were the most important days. The days that fueled my desire to do the work and the days my teammates needed my encouragement the most.

It taught me a lot about teamwork and how your team is only as strong as its weakest link. The weakest link being me, or so I thought.

However, I was just as important as anyone else on the team.

I made it my mission that first season to be their encourager, supporter, and biggest fan. I wanted them to know that just because I couldn't play didn't mean I didn't care. In fact, it made me fall in love with the game even more.

Coach Cap not only gave me a chance for a new beginning when he recruited me for Rockhurst University, he also gave me the gift of teaching me that you can turn your circumstances around and use them to encourage others. I did go on to play golf competitively in the following seasons after the broken blessing of my wrist injury.

Having a supportive coach who encouraged me to look beyond myself only lit a fire in me to be more determined than ever to overcome any obstacle that was put in my path while also encouraging others.

Without the valuable lessons, support, and motivation from him to keep going, I could have easily quit and let a horrible bump in the road discourage me from my true path. Instead, he did what great coaches do; he believed in me when I doubted myself. His belief in me allowed me to learn to believe in myself more.

For that, along with his grace, I am forever thankful that he saw potential in me long before I saw potential in myself.

TODAY IS THE DAY

October 5, 2001

Today is the day
It is rainy
But I'm smiling
I'm going to do well
Try my best
Get taped up
And prepared
Stretch
Everyone watch
And beware
I'm ready
To swing
And do my thing
I'm going to play
All day
For I am excited
And nothing is in my way
Watch out
Here I come
This is my game
And this isn't
About fame
Golf is everything
Not just something
I'm happy
I'm going to play

LESSON OF GROWTH

Dr. Darden

Rockhurst University, freshman year. Academically my focus was there, yet my grades were not reflecting my endless hard work and study efforts. I was struggling not only academically but in every other aspect.

Here I was in college, with no support system, and I wasn't able to play golf due to my recent wrist injury.

I was devastated. I didn't know what to do, so Coach Cap suggested I seek the help of a counselor in the counseling center. I met with a female counselor a couple of times, but she felt that another licensed psychologist who worked in the counseling center would be a better fit due to our shared sports backgrounds, and because she felt with the complexities of my struggles between academics and golf, he would be better equipped to help me work through it all.

She introduced me to Dr. Darden and we scheduled our first session.

During our first meeting I sat in the chair and curled myself up into a tight little ball, avoiding eye contact by hiding my face. As Dr. Darden describes it: "When you did look at me, your eyes looked like a scared little kid who was afraid that she might be in some kind of trouble!"

That's how I felt — like I had done something wrong — and that was why I was sent to Dr. Darden.

I was scared and I didn't know what to think. Now I had to learn to trust this man, hoping he wouldn't abandon me by making someone else "deal" with me.

I was hurt, and felt completely lost. I had no idea what to do. So I sat in silence.

When our time was up he insisted on scheduling another session, and I hesitantly agreed. He communicated to me that he was there to help me and that he understood it might take time for me to trust him. He asked that I give him a chance, as he wanted to help so that I could grow. He explained that if it meant sitting in silence until I felt comfortable to open up and talk, then so be it. That is what we would do.

It did take a few weeks and many silent moments for me to begin to open up and build a student/counselor relationship with Dr. Darden. Once I trusted him, there was no shutting me up, as I had a lot to say.

He would always welcome me with such a delightful and most positive "Hello!" During our sessions, he sat in his blue chair while I sat in another chair. Sometimes I sat curled up and sometimes like a normal human being. With a big grin on his face, he would ask "How is Miss Erin today?" every single time.

There were times I was in a great mood, then there were moments I would cry, be angry, upset, or at my wits' end. Regardless, he would listen. He never once told me what to do.

Being impatient for guidance, I was always looking for answers or approval and acceptance, and a "way to go!" for my accomplishments. Yet he didn't always make it that easy. However, he became one of my biggest supporters and cheerleaders during my college years.

Dr. Darden always had a way to go deeper, beyond the surface of my problems. He would guide me in exploring my past while teaching me skills that would prepare me for the future. He did his best to help me remain patient and in the present. That was always challenging for me and I continue to work on it to this day.

He was able to get me to understand and be open to the most difficult of areas within my life by comparing it to my beloved golf.

He challenged me to look at things from different perspectives and asked very specific questions: "Why?" Or "How come?"

Then instead of giving me the answers, he would insist I already knew the answers myself. He was able to teach me the art of self-thought, which led to self-discovery, and ultimately, how to always keep growing. Without growth I would have remained stuck in a constant battle of uncertainty.

Through our sessions he inspired me to grab hold of my own life and to not let my circumstances control my capabilities.

Whenever we would dive into uncomfortable territory I would immediately shut down. As hard as he would try to get me to engage in discussions, sometimes I denied them altogether, to avoid the discomfort and change the direction of the conversation. Then I avoided our next session by just not scheduling it. When I decided I was ready to talk about it, I would come back prepared with my answers and be open to diving deeper. He always knew when I just needed time, a moment to step back and reflect on my own.

After all, that's how I have always operated. I don't do anything until I am absolutely ready and sure I can handle it. I am getting better, though, when it comes to avoidance. Thanks to Dr. Darden I have developed self-awareness with a desire for growth.

In all of our many sessions he reminded me that it's not his place to judge, but rather it's his desire to help me accept myself by becoming the person I was always meant to be. His goal was for me to see my potential and to constantly seek growth.

His whole purpose was to show me through my own eyes how my imperfect past can always lead me to a beautiful future, if I desire to overcome my obstacles by always seeking growth. To never stop and always ask *Why*?

In one of our sessions I was describing myself and my life the way I saw it. Diving into the past felt like I was the onion, constantly a disappointment, and peeling away the dysfunctional layers of myself; it was messy.

He confidently and undeniably disagreed. He said yes, my life is like an onion, but I am not the onion. I was confused. He simply looked at me and proceeded to tell me that it was not how he saw me in the slightest. I asked him, "What other way could it be?"

He explained that though my life hadn't been perfect – that it had been inarguably dysfunctional and non-ideal – I was still standing with all that I had endured. I hadn't let it define me. That I had the capacity of taking something so raw, broken, and unimaginable and making it into something spectacular.

He said that my life had been difficult, yet I was not the onion. I had taken my circumstances and turned them into something beautiful, a pearl. I didn't quite get it then and I definitely didn't agree with him.

Throughout my life I was constantly given the message of not being good enough, pretty enough, smart enough, so how the hell was I going to think I could be comparable to a pearl, of all things?

A pearl! That conversation has always stuck with me. It wasn't until a decade later I started grasping this analogy of his where I am the pearl, and now I actually understand it.

During my first year in college I had an array of struggles and obstacles thrown at me. Without his persistence to guide me, I don't think I would have done as well as I did.

After my wrist injury from golf and not being able to play, I decided to throw myself into my academics full time. However, another health barrier got in my way.

College was hard; it's nothing like high school. Adjusting to the academics was extremely difficult for me. I didn't party or drink. I studied, studied, and studied some more. Not only did I go to school full time, I worked full time, and I was on the golf team. Though I couldn't play, I went to every practice. I went to bed at 9 p.m. every night and woke up at 5 a.m. every day. It was just the way I operated. I am happy to say that to this day I have yet to ever pull an all-nighter.

I also got involved with a campus organization to motivate and encourage students. The organization wasn't growing, but I got involved to see if I could make a difference. Within a few weeks, I was coming up with ideas and solutions to improve student engagement, and they were working. Soon, I was elected President of the organization, and my first order of business was to change the name. The name was PLUS (Peers Listening, Understanding and Supporting), and it didn't represent what we were all about. Therefore, I suggested the name PEERS, which stands for Positively Educating Each Rockhurst Student. The name changed the entire university's view of the organization! PEERS still operates today.

With everything I had going on, the pressure was building, yet I felt I could handle it.

My first semester was finally coming to a close, which meant lots of studying and finals. I was done, exhausted, and at my wits' end, but also very much in denial. I decided to stop in to the counseling center. I sat down and just started talking about all the things I had to do.

Dr. Darden looked at me and said, "You seem stressed?"

I abruptly and defensively said, "I am not stressed!" With my mouth tightly clenched I threw my arms up in the air, then let them slam down by my sides, hitting the cushions beneath me.

Dr. Darden, wide-eyed and with a smile on his face said, "OK, you're not stressed."

Soon after, I left. I took a little nap and then it was time for dinner. I made my way up to the cafeteria and decided to make a plate of fettuccini alfredo. As I made my way into the dining hall, I found a friend and sat down to join her.

Tired and just not feeling well, I took a look at her and then my plate. I slowly put my fork into my pasta dish and took a bite. As I chewed and then swallowed my food, I began to shake uncontrollably. My friend looked at me and asked if I was OK. I really didn't know. Tears welled up in my eyes as the shaking got worse.

She calmly looked at me and suggested that we go to the bathroom and throw some water on my face. I barely nodded my head yes, and as I slowly rose out of my chair I took a step back and suddenly collapsed. Before my head hit the floor, my friend Jarrod caught me as he was walking by.

Next thing I knew I was lying on the floor, confused, shaking and crying. Before I had a chance to get up, the paramedics had arrived and were assessing my condition.

I was rushed to the emergency room, where doctors began a bunch of tests. Jarrod rode in the front seat of the ambulance and stayed at the hospital with me until I was released later that evening.

After my emergency room visit, I was frightened and could no longer deny the level of stress I was experiencing. The next day, I checked in with Dr. Darden and told him what had happened. He looked at me again with that smile of his and said, "Guess you weren't stressed, huh?" followed by both of us laughing. After that point, I made it a priority to talk to him on a regular basis. I was in his schedule permanently.

I was advised by the emergency room doctor to follow up with my primary doctor, and was eventually referred to a cardiologist. At 19 years old.

The cardiologist ran tests and I was diagnosed with arrhythmia. My heart rate was under 60 beats per minute (bpm). When it fell below 50 bpm, and my stress levels were high, I would have what they referred to as "an episode." However, because of my young age, the cardiologist kept running tests throughout the next two years. Eventually it was discovered the arrhythmia was actually due to an underlying issue.

Due to constantly having fainting episodes, my cardiologist had decided it would be best to run one more test, called the table tilt test. There were only two ways this could go, positive or negative.

Here I was, a couple years into college and having fainting spells. Sometimes, there would be no warning and I would go down. Other times, if I could feel one coming on, I would be able to immediately take my medication, which ultimately made me have to go to bed. Therefore, the table tilt test was our last option of figuring out a cause so we could better manage the spells.

To do the test, I was strapped to a table and raised up in the air at different angles. They started me at 90 degrees and then put me at 80 degrees and then 70. When I hit the 70-degree mark, I didn't feel well, and within seconds it was lights out. The next thing I knew I was lying down as I had originally started and the doctor was next to me saying that we had our answer. The results were positive. I felt nauseous and sick as if I was about to throw up. I didn't, luckily.

It was scary; however, we had a diagnosis: neurocardiogenic syncope, also known as vasovagal syncope. The best way I can describe it is miscommunication between the heart and brain, and the body is told to shut down and to restart the heart. Not a fun thing! It was terrifying.

Soon I was back in the cardiologist's office and we began discussing preventatives to help me better control my new-found life, as I like to put it. My doctor encouraged me to take this extremely seriously, and because I was young it was better to start now and make some changes part of my everyday routine.

He explained that regular exercise, discontinuing my beta blocker, and eating a higher salt diet would help keep my blood volume up. I should also drink more water daily, stop consuming caffeinated beverages, as well as avoid stressful situations. This was my best plan of action. So that's what I did!

Dr. Darden helped me navigate new ways to reduce my stress. Being outside, writing, and taking regular naps would help me de-stress and be my saving grace. These activities kept me focused and less stressed. It was hard enough keeping a tight schedule, but making sure I added those things to it helped me stay healthy.

A new challenge and a new way of doing things is hard sometimes for a 19-year-old, so thank goodness for the wonderful and priceless resources I had available at Rockhurst University.

I struggled with many different things throughout my four years of college, and if it wasn't for Dr. Darden helping me navigate through them, I really don't know how I would have survived.

He has always been a big part of my life since the day I sat silent in the big blue chair in his office, curled up like a little girl who thought she was in trouble. Though I am out of college, and though he is no longer my counselor, I think of him often, update him when I am able, and visit him whenever I am in town. He may have been my counselor in college, but today I consider him a mentor and friend. For he so gracefully showed me how to look within myself, and planted a desire to grow, to never stop learning, and to always trust myself, because I ultimately already had the answer.

To this day, any time I thank Dr. Darden, he always says the same thing. "*You* are the one who made the big difference, not me. It was your willingness to engage and do the work while you were here as well as during the years that followed that has had the greatest influence on the woman you are today!"

Thank you again, Dr. Darden, for showing me the way by giving me the desire to always seek growth.

A HOLE-IN-ONE KIND OF LESSON

My Mom

Golf has taught me invaluable lessons that I will never take for granted. My mother never understood it until she read my golf journal, a collection of all my scorecards, schedules, practice rounds, self-written notes, and articles highlighting my skills on the golf course. She then made her own notes and found peace within my journey and understood why the game means so much to me.

Reading her notes and seeing how she expressed her thoughts in metallic ink on little black Post-it notes scattered throughout my golf journal has solidified the self-acceptance that she taught me, along with the invaluable lessons from those family and friends I was lucky enough to call my golf mentors!

Years ago, when she first wrote those words, I was angry because I didn't understand how she could be supportive through Post-it notes, but not with words or actions when I was actually actively participating in the game during my younger years. However, now reading the following only lets me see more clearly how she viewed me both as a golfer and then as her daughter.

My mother's notes in my golf scrapbook:

Give her wings and watch her fly!

Wow! Look at all those birdies!!!

Better watch out Chan! – She's catching up!!!

Getting Ready to Play at the Cameron Tournament.

Missouri Golf! The "Show-Me" State and she did!

Great Job Erin! I am Proud of you!

And her scores get better!

And we all have our eye on Erin Bush…

WOW

And Better!

She's getting pretty close! And it's not luck!

Watch out! Here she goes!

She has stuck to it and she keeps getting better and her persistence is going to pay off….

One fine day, while the sun is shining, and the sky is blue…. And little white balls become like birds…. Flying through the air after being hit square with great calm and great follow thru – we will all put our hands to shade our eyes so that we can see who this girl is – the one carrying her bag – the bag that says: GOLF IS NOT A GAME OF PERFECT!

Jr. Year – now she's getting serious…

And the other teams know her name after the first match...

The other coaches are keeping their eyes on this new girl!

Never Listen to Never.

Do not let those thoughts inside. You know you can DO THIS – LET ME TELL YOU A SECRET, SHH!!! The people who tell you negative stuff or laugh while you are saying something serious. They don't have any creativity or determination – they wield fear like a knife, they are insecure, this is their problem. Your Dad always says – IT IS YOU and that LITTLE WHITE BALL – when it comes down to it, it's you + your confidence and hard work. Your determination and your imagination will and already have begun to blend from within. Once you feel right and realize we are behind you 1 million % + some me, your dad, others too.

REMEMBER

GOLF IS NOT A GAME OF PERFECT!

AND ALSO

People are not perfect = but they like to play games...

2 Girls – that makes it tough!

But you saw it through!

WOW! The 1st Letter!

Erin, a small, but strong lady Tiger pulls in

> the best score for the Lady Tigers time & time again – she has a beautiful swing!
>
> Like father...like daughter, what a pair!

This next section is what brings TEARS to my eyes each and every time:

> I know it's been a lonely sport for you — but you have stuck with it — it is in your blood and it calls to you. I am PROUD OF YOU! Keep going — you will get there!

Autograph section of Professional
LPGA Players:

> Erin – You need to add your Signature!
>
> I can see that almost against all odds you have stuck to Golf – I have great respect for you – you've had very little help – but I believe your ducks are lining up and they will turn into eagles and you will feel strong and comfortable with yourself and your game. The pieces are coming together because YOU are putting them together. I LOVE YOU.
>
> You have always been a master puzzle piecer! So, I know you can do this if you want! I am Proud of you Star Sweeper!

When I read and reflect on these words, I realize that my world may not have always been a game of perfect, but my world has been my own. A puzzle I have slowly put together and made mine. Golf is my rock; it is my consistency now just as it has always been. I have always reflected back on my own life through the eyes of a golfer, a master puzzler, and a girl who has always just wanted to make those around her proud. Even when I read those words today, they pierce me to my heart. They get me out of a deep bunker of self-doubt and open my eyes to the acceptance of all the lessons I have learned up to this point. But as history repeats itself, so do the lessons that I have learned in so many ways.

I love golf! There is no question about that. I have established a relationship with the sport rather than it being a sport I just play.

Besides my relationship with my dad and my golf buddies, I didn't have any other *dependable* relationships with people my age. However, golf was my rock; it was never-changing, it was consistent and it was something I could hold onto. Therefore, I formed a bond with golf. I began giving golf human characteristics. However, I actually didn't realize this until now, while writing my story.

Looking back, I knew golf was my only constant and it never let me down – I got it right and I fell deeply in love with it. It became my very first obsession. Golf had taken on the role of a relationship. Dan, Dick, Coach Cap, Dr. Darden and they all saw that I had a love for the game.

They were able to utilize golf to teach me very valuable lessons of patience, integrity, encouragement, determination, and a desire to always grow, which allowed me to become the woman I am today.

They took what I already knew about golf and related it to my life, so that I could analyze life when necessary and take the shot when needed to understand myself, my purpose, and to live life fully.

It was also the bond that my dad and I had, the thing that connected us when we were miles apart; the thing that we could call ours.

Golf is the one thing I have always relied on, that I could call my own and go back to when I needed to feel important or *enough* when I wasn't sure. I could always go to the course.

For me, golf is so much more than just a sport or a game you play. It has helped me learn about love, loss, disappointment, happiness, hazards, goals, dreams, and miracles. It teaches me about life every time I connect with the ball. It teaches me about highs and lows, easy shots and challenging ones, both in the game and in life.

It taught me that you have to take one shot at a time.

Keeping score is important but it's not the only thing.

Golf taught me that the mind is a powerful tool.

You have to enjoy it all, because if you don't, at the end of the round you may regret the risks you didn't take and the times you played it safe. Isn't that true with life as well?

Golf taught me that the simplest shot may be the most complicated, and how even if you make mistakes and end up in some hazardous situation, you can always recover, learn a lesson, and move on.

Golf has always been my greatest gift, life lesson, and my most unswerving blessing; my biggest cheerleader. The one relationship I have made my own and always got right.

Golf to me is not a game of perfect, but rather a pure example of what life has to offer.

Life, a game we play in all conditions whether naturally skilled or not — is one you can learn as you go. You have good shots and bad, and it is up to you whether you keep playing or give up.

Chapter 3

The Tipping Point – The Abuse

2008 – World of Isolation

THE DAY

March 28, 2001

Today the sky sheds its tears for it knows
As much as the wind blows
What you've been through
For the pain you've been through is so immense
That you cannot explain
While the day breaks
You try to forget
And your reasons are true for what you have told

The afternoon comes as you try to smile
And then leaves after a little while
The day will go but you remember
Even though it is no longer
Memories are made and some forgotten
People share and others just don't care
The day ends and nightfall begins
For we eat then we go to bed
Where we lay our heads
And begin to sleep
For many count all the sheep
We dream of fairies and other things too
But most of all you dream of you
So, sleep tight
And remember the days when everything was fine
And seemed okay
Because those are important, especially for you
Because remember those are the ones you made it
through

The Tipping Point, or *The Day,* as this poem is titled, didn't come for many years after this was written. Then, I was just a girl in high school who had been abandoned by everyone she held dear to her except a select few. Eight years after the poem was written came The Day when I finally stood up for myself to a man who was no man, but a monster who abused and raped me.[1]

1. If you are in danger, contact the National Domestic Violence Hotline: 1-800-799-7233.

I will admit it; I had no idea that abuse was so common. Why would I? I didn't know anyone who had been a victim of domestic violence, sexual assault, verbal or emotional abuse… or did I?

Here's the thing, how would I know if someone close to me was or had been a victim of abuse? The only way would be if I was educated on the subject, witnessed the abuse, or if friends had confided in me about their abuse, right?[2]

It's a topic that is not touched on or taught about in school. However, it should be, especially with the statistics that exist in our country today. As of this printing, women make up 50.6 percent of 332,015,736 people in the United States.[3]

That's over 168 million women that make up the United States population. What does that mean? According to the Domestic Violence Hotline,[4] it means that approximately 41 million women in the US will be abused at some time in their lifetime. That's unacceptable!

What I considered my first experience with abuse happened during my college years. I met a guy who wanted to be my boyfriend when I was a freshman in college. I was 18 and so naïve.

I thought I was an adult — after all, I could take care of myself; I had been doing it since the age of 14.

---

2. To learn more about the red flags of domestic or sexual abuse, see https://www.thehotline.org.

3. Countrymeters https://countrymeters.info/en/United_States_of_America_(USA).

4. The National Domestic Violence Hotline https://www.thehotline.org/resources/statistics/

Wrong! I wasn't educated about what *red flags* to look out for when it came to abuse.

For me, "abuse" meant physical violence, and I wasn't experiencing that, so I was fine. Wrong again! My first experience with abuse was both verbal and emotional.

The emotional and mental abuse hurts a hell of a lot more than the bruises ever could. Why? The scars left behind from verbal and emotional abuse are deep, and covered, hidden from view. They ruin you.

Sometimes you don't even know they are there until years down the road. They are the worst kind of scar. They stay with you; they haunt you and they manipulate your mind.

That relationship lasted for only six months, but the damage had been done. I was in counseling, and while I thought I had healed, I was far from it.

I fell into abusive relationship after abusive relationship. Each one was worse than the last. They don't always have to be with someone you are dating. They can be with people you consider friends or family.

Fast forward seven years to when I experienced physical abuse for the first time. I was in denial — a young woman who had no idea how badly my world was spinning out of control.

I was living in Missouri at the beginning of 2008. I had just completed my master's program at Avila University, was working at Barnes and Noble Booksellers, and applying for jobs of interest within the golf industry.

That January, I had the opportunity to attend the PGA Merchandise Show in Orlando, Florida.

I invested every extra penny I had into that opportunity.

On the first day of the show, I was nervous as all get out. But as I waited for the bus to take me to the Show, a man walked up to me and said "You look lost!" I responded with, "I am!"

His name was Rich, and he is still a very good friend of mine. I was 25 years old, in town for a convention, and I was lost. He was kind and asked me what my goals were, and I explained to him with youthful excitement, "To find a job and get myself out of Missouri!" He obliged and showed me the ropes.

The convention lasted for three glorious days and he was there every step of the way. I am forever grateful!

With my professional attire, resume, and contact card in hand, I was armed for success. I figured I had nothing to lose and I would wing it. Instead, Rich told me that all I had to do was walk up to the right person, introduce myself, give a firm handshake, and demand a job. He told me, "Don't let them forget who you are!"

Was he kidding? No, he was quite serious, and he never led me astray that weekend. I did exactly as he instructed and made great contacts, went home with a stack of business cards, and set myself up for my dream career.

I made it back home to miserable Kansas City, which connected me to my past. There was so much concrete, I felt confined within the city limits.

I began contacting everyone I had met in Orlando and thanked them for the opportunity to speak with them. I eagerly applied for jobs and patiently waited for responses while I continued to work at the bookstore.

Because of Rich, I gained the courage to let people know who I am and not to let anyone forget me. Rich and I became good friends, and he always tells me to keep my tenacity and never give up on my dreams!

The Executive Director of the Colorado PGA called to inform me there was a job and I should apply.

I did!

I had a phone interview and the waiting began.

Unfortunately, I wasn't picked for the job, and I was devastated. At this point my mom and I had been speaking for a couple of years. I just needed her.

I went to my mother's apartment later that morning and she couldn't believe it. After all, she had helped me with my application, cover letter, and resume.

She told me, "They made a mistake! You are supposed to get that job!" I tried to explain to her that something else would come my way.

Two weeks went by, and I couldn't believe it — I got another call from the Executive Director from the Colorado Section of the PGA.

He started out by explaining how they had made a mistake, and they would like to offer me a job, but I needed to be out there by the end of the week.

The end of the week? I was working, and I didn't have time to give the bookstore a two-week notice. *Oh no!*

What was I going to do? All I could do was listen to my gut. I accepted the job!

I packed, informed Mrs. Haney of my move, and I was on my way across the country towards Colorado to start my life.

I drove 12 hours west, landed an apartment, unpacked, and got settled in. On Monday I started my new position as Operations Manager. I was ecstatic!

Here I was, 25 years old and I had my dream job. Not just a job, a career. I oversaw all operations and golf day events for the Colorado PGA.

I was doing an amazing job and my team, the professional golfers, the board of directors and golf course managers loved me! I was finally being accepted.

Before I took it over, the Women and Golf Day event was not very successful and usually had a low turnout. I wasn't about to let that happen again.

I worked long and hard to prepare for that event with only 30 days or so before it took place. I called, emailed, and reached out to every single contact I had made just months before at the PGA Merchandise Show.

Everyone wanted in, they wanted to get involved, and they did! I raised over $2,500 in sponsorships, and over $1,500 in prizes and giveaways. I was able to get women-owned companies involved and participants were eagerly signing up! It was a very successful and amazing day. I loved it!

I had met someone, too! A PGA apprentice who volunteered his time for the Women and Golf Day event. We started dating.

You guessed it — the monster.

The relationship started out like any other relationship: he liked me, I liked him, let's date. Before I knew it, he was moving into my apartment just a few months after we met and I was completely confused about why he thought he could move in without discussion . . . and why I allowed it. I was manipulated and didn't even know it.

He began taking advantage of me, not helping me with bills, and telling me how to dress. He dictated how I should act and what I could and could not do. We would fight. He began restraining me, hitting me, and beating me. I took it. *What else could I do?* He was bigger than me — I was a measly 100 pounds. It was frightening and I was ashamed. He would apologize and give me any and all excuses for me to forgive him. He told me he didn't mean it, that he cared about me. He also said I was unlovable, and I should be so lucky because he loved me. I forgave him.

Once he forced me out of a moving golf cart at top speed. Back then they moved pretty fast. I fell to the grass beneath the cart, rolled, and still finished the round. I had no other choice. What was I going to do? He was my ride and he lived with me.

When we went out, he would drink, flirt with other women, and then beat me at home. Then the following morning or evening he would bring me red roses as if that would make it all OK. He would even say, "I'm sorry, I love you, it will never happen again." I believed him over and over again.

But it did, and each time it was worse than the last. I was trapped. To this day, I hate red roses.

On Halloween night, it was snowing, he was DJ'ing and had had too much to drink. I somehow made him angry at me, I don't even know what for. He made a scene outside. It was awful and embarrassing. People were staring! One person could tell I needed help, he even approached the car, but the monster threatened him so he walked away. But I was helpless and people didn't help; they walked away after the monster drunkenly yelled and told me to get in the car. We got home, and he passed out. I was exhausted, and did my best to fall asleep. In the morning he again arrived with red roses and apologized.

It was awful. He did horrible things. Not only did he verbally, emotionally, physically abuse me but he *raped me*!

Rape is a horrible thing, a demoralizing, excruciatingly painful act. When it is happening all you can do is numb yourself, praying it will stop. You can try to fight back and I did, I tried, but he pinned me to the bed with every ounce of force he could. My face pushed into the bed, my arms stretched out and pinned by each of his hands around my wrists and his disgusting body pressed against mine. He penetrated every ounce of my innocence. This monster, who I tried to convince myself cared for me, this monster who always apologized and promised he wouldn't hurt me, he deflated me over and over again until there was nothing of me left. I eventually got a hand free, found an object and threw it at him, hoping to make it all stop. It stopped, but the damage had been done. I got away, but I couldn't escape. He grabbed me, he beat me, and I froze, covering my face and head. After the beating stopped I stayed in the bedroom, crying myself to sleep. I had never felt so ashamed, dirty and scared.

Rape is painful; it's demeaning and it breaks your soul.

It shatters your existence into a million little pieces and you have no idea how to pick them up and glue them back together in hopes of making it look whole again. The scars of rape run deep, they are ugly and they burn. They never go away.

After the rape, we were evicted from the apartment. The neighbors complained of yelling, screaming, and arguing. They could hear everything! Instead of getting help, now I was in search of a new place, hoping he wouldn't follow. He did. Here we were in a new apartment and I was scared as ever. I didn't know what else to do, so I stayed.

Christmas was coming and we were invited to his friend's party, which meant drinking and not a good night for me. When we decided to leave, he was drunk and stumbling all over the place. I helped him into the car, and I drove home. When we arrived, he pushed me out of the car onto the icy driveway. It was bad. I slipped and then caught my balance. Before I made my way upstairs, I pulled into the garage. Once again he passed out, and I went to bed saddened by what my world was. I didn't know what to do. I felt more isolated with each passing day. But this was my life and he loved me because he said so. I believed him.

I hated myself.

To top it off, I had my dream career and I lost it!

I didn't do anything wrong, I was great at my job, but I wasn't able to keep the bruises and signs of abuse hidden even though I thought I had. I remember going into the conference room where my coworkers confronted me, and I just denied it all. I wasn't a victim of abuse; I would never be in that situation. "How could you question my relationship, don't you know I am a grown woman?"

They were concerned, but I felt attacked. The thing is, every aspect of my life at that time was unhealthy for me. My world was falling apart and I was alone more than ever. Even the person who was my boss, he too was abusive (verbally and emotionally), so it was best I lost my job. The reason they gave was "restructuring of the section."

My boss and coworkers at the time recognized the signs of a victim of abuse, and instead of helping me they let me go, abandoned me, and left me to my own traumas. Abandonment was no stranger to me. *Why would this be any different?*

They were right, I needed to take care of myself. I had no idea where to start. Pretending everything was OK was easier. I had lost all sense of who I was and I felt stuck. Stuck in this hell hole that was dark and not one ounce of light penetrated it, not one.

Because I lost my job, I needed a new one. I decided to apply at the gym. I was desperate. I had bills to pay, and the monster, the person who was supposed to love me, my partner at the time, well, he was no help. He was a drunk and an abuser, though I was in extreme denial. I just wanted to be loved, so I did everything I could to survive. And survival mode became my default. I didn't dare ask for anything. After all, he reminded me regularly that I should be grateful that someone like him could love someone like me.

I marched into my gym, went straight to the manager, and pleaded for a job. They could see my desperation; I started the next day. Finally, I had a reason to escape, even if it was for minimum wage and for a few hours; it was better than being in a room with the monster.

I needed money and I needed it now. I took every job I could. Working all the time kept me from feeling my feelings, it kept me in survival mode, and it kept me from facing reality. I worked, I slept, I worked, I got beaten, I cried, I slept, and I repeated it just to survive, hoping one day I would be saved. But I knew no one was coming to save me. It was a false dream.

After a few weeks working at the gym, I met a strong, independent, and beautiful woman.

She embraced me immediately and hired me as an executive assistant. She was self-employed, which I found fascinating.

She was one of the most amazing, smart, and strong women I had ever met. If it wasn't for her giving me an opportunity and sharing her life experiences with me, I am not sure how my life would have turned out.

She was working on a speech for a workshop she was hosting and she needed me to do some research. I told her that I would be happy to. The topic: domestic violence. Let me remind you, I was still in this horribly abusive relationship. She knew it but didn't say anything; she just knew.

I split my time between her office and my apartment. While the monster was at work, I did the research. I will never forget the day I realized I was in an abusive relationship.

I was sitting at my computer researching *signs* and *red flags* in reference to domestic violence in relationships. As I went through the list, I checked them off one by one. I sat there frozen, scared, alone, and shocked most of all. I questioned everything within my mind. I tried to justify it. He always told me he loved me and everything was my fault. He made me question my behavior, my actions, and made me think I was crazy, so it must have been my fault, right? He manipulated me so much that I believed *I* was the problem. All of the questions led to confusion. I became awakened and lost all at the same time. I didn't know what to do or who I was.

The only thing I knew to do was to call her. Call her and confess. She didn't say much; she didn't have to. That was my first educational lesson on abuse. It got me thinking and trying to figure things out.

I was frozen. *Now what?* Being aware of my situation, my terrible situation, I had to do something if I was going to survive. I still pretended everything was OK.

I began to read a book that my father had read and then sent to me to read, *The Gift of Fear* by Gavin de Becker. He knew I was in a bad situation, not because I told him; he also just knew.

I was paralyzed with the turning of each page. Horrified and trapped in a never-ending storm.

A storm of a terrifying reality that I never could have imagined would be my own, yet here I was and it all came crashing down.

I will never forget it: January 23, 2009.

On that day, my life changed. I was scheduled for a double shift at the gym. I was there at 5 a.m. and my friend and coworker was begging me to get out of my abusive relationship. He was the only person I confided in. When anyone else asked, I denied it.

On my way home on a break between shifts, something snapped. My friend from work was right, but how? *How was this possible? How did this happen? Was this the best that my life would be?* I was only 26 years old and stuck in a relationship I thought would never end.

I was terrified, because what I was planning on doing could be life-changing or could be the end of my existence.

I pulled into my garage, walked up the stairs and found the monster in my bathrobe, a weird habit of his, gambling online with money he wouldn't use to help with bills. Ignoring me in my own home. Something flipped deep inside me and I totally lost it. I went mad. Bat-shit crazy!

I began to empty the kitchen island drawers of his things, dumping them into trash bags. At first, he just kept gambling, and then started to watch. It was weird. I didn't really notice until he started following me.

I made my way to the bedroom, gathered his clothes from the closet, and began tossing them angrily down the stairs that I had just climbed. Anything that was his had to go, all of it down the stairs. I was on a rampage.

He didn't like what I was doing. I was making my way to the living room, when suddenly I ran right into him. He grabbed my wrists, tightly. It hurt and I couldn't get out of his grip. I started pounding his chest with my clenched fists as he fought. I yelled at him with rage, "Get Out! Get Out!" over and over and over again. Then he released me. But the beating was about to begin.

I had a heart condition, and was desperately looking for my phone. I found it. I was trying to discreetly call 911, but he appeared again and took the phone from me. He grabbed me again, took me to the closet and threw me to the floor. He started kicking me repeatedly until I was in the corner, where he continued to kick me.

I just laid there, head covered, in fetal position. It stopped, and he phoned my twin sister. I could hear him very clearly. He began speaking in a calm tone. "Erin is having an 'episode,'" he explained to my sister. I was crying and having an anxiety attack. I didn't know what was going to happen to me. It didn't matter what he called it, because I was praying in that moment that my sister would hear me screaming, but she didn't. My heart condition was getting worse. He hung up, standing over me with a look of evil in his eyes. I begged him for my phone. I pleaded, gasping for air, my heart pounding. I needed to call my doctor.

He threw the phone at me, told me to stay there. He left, slamming the door behind him.

I didn't move, just as the monster had ordered. I was so terrified, but I did phone my friend from work, the one I had been talking to just before I had left earlier that day.

I quietly told him what was going on, and almost before I knew it, he was there at my door hoping to keep the monster I had allowed into my unraveling life away from me.

I didn't know where the monster was, but while my friend stayed with me, the monster called his mother (though he was 41 years old) begging her to talk some sense into me. I told her not to come over, but she arrived several minutes later.

My friend kept the monster and his mother confined to the bottom of the stairs. He told them to gather the pile that I had created at the bottom of the stairs and to leave, to never come back.

I finally stood up for myself, standing outside with my friend keeping me safe, and told the monster's mother, "No, I want him out!" She was only mildly shocked, because she knew I was done and there was no pleading with me.

In that moment of bravery, after they had left, I didn't recognize myself standing tall in that apartment. The only thing I knew was that I had some fight in me. The beating he had just given me was the tipping point.

I declared in my soul that day that I would never be physically beaten again, by him or by anybody else.

I didn't go back to work that day. I stayed locked in my apartment with my friend watching over me. I was scared and exhausted, but that was just the beginning of my fight for my life.

January came and went; February was awful because I was living in fear; now March was halfway over. It was March 19, 2009 and I had no idea how one phone call could change the direction of my life forever.

The monster's cats were still with me in my apartment, as he refused to get them. I felt he still had his grip on me through his pets. I didn't want that — I wanted to be done. I wanted nothing more than to move on.

Yes, I love animals, but these animals were like their owner, mean and not something I wanted in my life. Because they were a link to the monster, I wanted them out. I decided to call the animal shelter and ask for advice.

I remember introducing myself and informing the woman who answered that I had two cats in my possession that were not mine. They were my ex's and he kept refusing to come and take them. I kept asking if I could just "Open the door and let them outside?" I know how that sounds, but I was desperate.

She informed me I could be charged with animal neglect as the cats were in my care even though they were not my animals. As I begged for a solution, I let it slip that this man was dangerous and he had been abusive towards me physically and sexually. "Please just come and get the cats so I can move on."

I kept talking as I always did when I was nervous, but she stopped me mid-sentence. The lady asked me to repeat what I had just said and I asked her what she meant. I repeated myself, but it wasn't what she was referring to. She said to me in a calm but concerned manner, "What did you say before that?" I knew what she was asking, so in a panic I repeated to her how I had been abused by this man and I just wanted the cats gone. "I want to get on with my life."

Once I confirmed her suspicions, she told me I had to hold and that she was putting me in contact with the police department. She informed me that even if I hung up, they would be contacting me regardless, as per Colorado State Law she was in a position of mandatory reporting and my case was to be reported. She had all my information, so I stayed on the line.

Staying on the line waiting for an officer to pick up on the other end, I stood there in shock and disbelief. I was frightened for what was to come. I had no idea what my future looked like, but this, all of this couldn't be happening, could it?

An officer of the Douglas County Police Department got on the line. I was scared! I informed the officer on the phone of what had happened and what my current situation was. I asked if all of this was necessary, if they could forget all about it. They denied my request. The fear set in even deeper.

I filed a police report on March 23, 2009, in the back room of the gym where I worked. I wasn't sure what was going to happen and how I would ever get through it. I cried. I was scared and beyond embarrassed. I was ashamed of the girl who sat there in the back room feeling completely alone and utterly disappointed. *How did I let this happen?* This was the question that went through my mind as I sifted through the horrific moments I had been through. Having to write them down and put them on paper was terrifying. Because when those memories of the beatings are locked up in your mind, you can be in complete denial. However, the moment you open your mouth and speak the terrible memories back into existence, it gives them life once again. It is emotional, it's messy, and it's traumatizing as you relive it over and over again.

The information you are about to read is real and quoted directly from the police report. I have blacked out names and other information to protect those involved, including myself. There is no need to block out the monster's name as it's public record, but this is my story and he deserves no recognition of what he considered glory.

County Court, Douglas County
The People of Colorado
v.
Defendant: *******, ****** ******
Denver, CO 80205

The Court finds it is appropriate to issue this Protection Order pursuant of 18-1-1001 C.R.S., that it has jurisdiction over the parties and the subject matter; that the Defendant was personally served and given reasonable notice and opportunity to be heard; that the Defendant constitutes a credible threat to the life and health of the Protected Person(s); and sufficient cause exists for the issuance of a Protection Order.

The Court finds that the Defendant (X) is ( ) is not governed by the Brady Handgun Violence Prevention Act, 18 U.S.C. 922 (d)(8) and (g)(8).

Therefore, it is ordered that you the Defendant:

1. Shall not harass, molest, intimidate, retaliate against, or tamper with any witness to or victim of the acts you are charged with committing.
2. Shall vacate the home of the victim(s), stay away from the home of the victim(s), and stay away from any other location the victim(s) is/are likely to be found.
3. Shall refrain from contacting or directly or indirectly communicating with the victim(s).

4. Shall not possess or control a firearm or other weapon.
5. Shall not possess or consume alcoholic beverages or controlled substances.

Is further ordered that:

This Order remains in effect until final disposition or further order of the Court. *

PLEASE NOTE: IMPORTANT NOTICES FOR DEFENDANT AND LAW INFORCEMENT OFFICIALS ON PAGE 2.

*Until final disposition of the action" means until the case is dismissed, until the Defendant is acquitted, or until the Defendant completes his/her sentence. Any Defendant sentenced to probation or incarceration shall be deemed to have completed his/her sentence upon discharge from probation or incarceration, as the case may be (18-1001(8)(b), C.R.S.)

Date: 3/19/2009

Judge

- Magistrate ELLIOT-DUMLER, BETH

Printed Name of Judicial Officer

By signing, I acknowledge receipt of this Order

Date: 3/30/2010

I certify that this is a true and complete copy of the original order

Date: 3/30/2010

JDF 440 R10/08 MANDATORY PROTECTION ORDER ISSUED PURSUANT TO 18-1-1001, C.R.S.

Please note: The above is my copy and it was received and acknowledged by the Defendant on March 30, 2010.

Approximately a year after the Protection Order was filed and received, and I completed the Victim Impact Statement, I had to be evaluated and assessed by the Crime Victim Compensation Board.

Things don't move very fast in the justice system. I wanted to be done, I wanted to move on, but for the next year and a half it would move at snail's pace.

The below is what I wrote on the Victim Impact Statement Form.

1. EFFECTS OF THIS CRIME ON YOU/YOUR FAMILY: Please describe injuries, costs, damages and overall effect of this crime on you, your family, and/or your business. Include fears, lifestyle changes, etc. attach additional pages as needed.

   The effects of this crime are horrendous. I fear for my life every day – emotionally I'm a mess. I have sought help to understand all the emotions that I'm going through. I have completely changed my routine – Mr. ******* knows a lot about me — where I work, how I come home — so I have completely changed my routine. I had my door locks changed; an alarm set in my apartment & I am always looking over my back.

I never thought I would live in fear. I never thought I would have to look over my shoulder every day. I never thought I would be scared.

But I do & I am.

Every morning I wake up I thank God I got through another night safely. I lock all my doors, windows to the outside world as well as lock myself in my room every night when I sleep.

I fear for my life — not only was I in danger when I was involved with Mr. ******* — I am still in danger now more than ever that I'm not involved.

I've changed everything so I may be just a little safer. As I said before I had the locks on my door changed both upstairs & down, I had my alarm set in my apartment and I have had my garage door opener reprogrammed all because I fear for my life.

Not only am I dealing with this inwardly — I've had to tell people about what's going on — just in case something happens. Mr. ******* — not only assaulted, harassed & abused me, but he took away my innocence, my ability to trust and replaced it with anger & fear. I am scared every day. I've not only been humiliated by communicating to friends & family — I have lost relationships with some of them — which were very important to me. For that I'm even more scared and feel very alone.

This is no way for me to live. I have no family here and the family I still talk to fear for my life every day.

I've sought help — but cannot afford it so every day I battle within myself emotions along with confusion. I constantly relive the horrible abusive & assaulting moments every day.

I have night terrors all the time. I cry, scream and freak out in my sleep — and because of this I don't sleep very well.

Sometimes I don't even understand my moods. I'll be having a good moment and then someone will ask me how I'm doing or how everything is going & I'll fall apart. I hate it.

I just want my life back — I want to be happy — but he took that away.

When I look into the mirror, I don't recognize the woman looking back. I'm a stranger to myself & it's his fault.

The things he did & said changed me and now I have to change just to get to know me again while living in fear.

I get sick just thinking about him and what he put me through — I battle with my health, and my heart condition, my mind and everything in between every day.

Trying to express on paper is a lot harder than how I feel, fear & live these days.

Please understand how I have been violated, how I fear for my life and how I battle every day.

If you have any questions please let me know.

This man deserves (and should be) to be punished.

As I said I have had to change everything.

*Above was copied word for word from the Victim Impact Statement.

The Crime Victim Compensation Board is responsible for processing a crime victim's request of financial losses (many areas fall under this) and approving or denying such claims. I was evaluated by a therapist at the Crisis Center that I was referred to and receiving help from.

The below information is derived from the Crime Victim Compensation Board Form that was completed on March 1, 2010, nearly a year later.

> Type of mental health coverage (Please indicate deductible amount and percentage insurance will pay per visit, per calendar year.)
>
> *Cigna Health Care as of January 1, 2011* (Note: coverage wouldn't start until following year)
>
> (Client is continuing with group therapy at this agency, every other week; she is now seeking weekly individual therapy close to her place of work in Boulder.)
>
> TREATMENT
>
> 1) Briefly describe victimization. (<u>Include date of crime, name of perpetrator and reporting law enforcement agency.)</u> Case opened 3/19/2009 after Douglas County investigator took perp's (******* ****** *******) cats to his house on call from Animal Shelter and he admitted to abusing victim, that she "deserved it." He was

arrested for hitting, raping, shoving, pushing and grabbing which occurred from 6/08/ through 12/08. On 10/31/08 perp pushed victim out of a stationary car onto an icy driveway. On 03/17/10, perp (******* *******) violated restraining order and caused victim to press charges, which brought up more court dates and emotional trauma.

B) Second Victims: None

2) What behavioral and emotional symptoms, directly relating to the victimization are currently being displayed by the patient/client? Depression, anxiety, nightmares, low self-esteem, distrust in men, body fatigue, under-eating, startle response to certain cues.
3) Clinical Diagnosis and code(s): (NOTE: The diagnosis should be based on the symptomology listed above.) **A DSM code must be included.**
   Axis i: 309.81 PTSD
   Axis ii: V71.09 No dx
   Axis iii:
   Axis iv: Victim of domestic abuse, chronic lack of consistent emotional support in childhood; childhood sexual abuse
   Axis v: 60
4) Compared to the client's current symptomology how was this person functioning prior to the crime? Client reports she was "feeling confident" – "nothing could stop me" "on top of

the world"; had a good career, no debt, none of the above symptoms except some mild stress.

5) Has the client/patient had previous mental health counseling?

x Yes _ No ___ Outpatient

If so, when? For 4 years in high school & college

Reason for treatment: Family problems

TREATMENT ISSUES

6) What are the treatment goals and objectives?
    - Address PTSD issues of anxiety, phobic reactions, nightmares, startle, distrust, depression
    - Process memories and effects of previous abuse by perpetrator
    - Discuss healthy relationships and reasons and possible propensities to get into abusive relationships
    - Help client regain self-esteem

Prognosis: Very good. Client is hard-working and motivated; PTSD and general anxiety are causing her lots of distress and she wants to resolve these issues.

7) Discuss treatment modalities used to achieve these goals.

Talk therapy and group therapy were primary modalities previously, EMDR was started (one preparatory session) but not completed due to client's moving and new job in Boulder. She would like to continue every other week group attendance here and has begun individual –

potentially EMDR — with a therapist in Boulder wherein she will access her insurance.

8) Describe any issue that may affect the length of treatment and effectiveness.
There may be a deeper history of childhood abuse than client is aware of at this time.

9) What other recommendations or treatment referrals might be made (i.e. psychological assessment, group therapy, psychological evaluation for medication)?
Combine both individual and group therapy. Individual will continue privately in Boulder.

10) Anticipated termination Date:
June 30th, 2011-(group only from 1/1/2011 until term date)

11) Date client entered treatment:
Client first seen for an intake on 4/1/2009 but not able to continue at that time; came back and began individual and group beginning 8/17/10
Number of sessions to date:
8 individual (all 2010) and 9 group
Please complete the section below:
8 Number of individual sessions at $80 per session
_ Number of family sessions at __per session
16 Number of group sessions at $40 per session

TOTAL COST OF TREATMENT: $640 + $640 = $1280

ADDITIONAL INFORMATION:
If so desired, please include additional information. Both the claimant and the therapist must sign this form.

I added my signature to both the copy I had and the one that was submitted, along with the therapist's signature. It felt like forever. I continued subsidized therapy to save money. I was into debt over $18,000 due to the abusive relationship I barely escaped from and was now receiving help so that I could recover. It was difficult. I wanted to do whatever was necessary to move on. I played Russian roulette with my bills, just hoping I could get by month after month.

Therapy was hard, both individually and in a group. Here I was, 27 years old and I was broken. Broken in every aspect of the word.

My mind, soul, and heart were shattered in a million pieces as a result of the abuse I endured. Sure, I was out of the relationship, but I had a difficult road ahead of me, and I didn't know where to begin. I just knew I needed to take one step at a time. Sometimes those steps seemed to be in quicksand and others felt like they were pushing me backwards.

The only thing I knew is I needed to lean on God, if he would have me. I was ripped away from Him through the abuse, but He never left my side. He didn't let me die in the arms of a monster. He picked me up and He did my fighting for me.

The day I threw my abuser out, it was not me who had spoken, but the little girl I was to protect and hadn't. I let her down and she picked me up, she raised her voice, and she fought for us. Because of the little girl inside me and God's grace for me, I was able to escape the hands of a monster one last time, which I would forever be grateful for.

When I look back to that time in my life, when I was manipulated, beaten, raped, and alone, it truly scares me. I know I escaped with not only my life, but a sliver of strength that gave me hope to become what I am today.

As people learn of my story, they typically ask if I wish that the abuse had never happened. Of course! However, the broken blessing is it has made me stronger and helped me understand true resiliency. Being abused was horrible, yet I can relate to so many others and give them hope. I can be an advocate. I can be a voice. God gives us battles and we have to decide if we are going to fight them or let our light be snuffed out.

I realized through my healing I have been able to connect with so many more women and show them the strength that they may not have to show themselves. I am grateful and humbled that I made it through the horrific acts that monster put me through. That God showed me strength, grace, and mercy to pull me through after such a mess, to inspire others.

I wish no one ever has to endure abuse, as it's awful and there is no way to truly explain the pain unless you too have been on that road. What breaks my heart the most is that many before me and many after me will be in similar or even worse situations and will feel alone, frightened, and hopeless. Making that phone call to the animal shelter was definitely a broken blessing. If it wasn't for that call, who knows what would have happened.

Many people don't understand how a woman finds herself in such an awful circumstance or dilemma. Many question victims of abuse and domestic violence, "Why don't you just leave? Why do you stay? Why do you put up with it?" The answer is anything but black and white.

It's complicated, and it's messy, and most of all we are blinded by the monsters who captured us. Unless you have been in an abusive relationship, you really don't see the grey area that lies between the black and white.

You are manipulated and deceived by this person you so willingly trusted, who turns on you over time. It doesn't happen overnight, or the next day, week, or month. It happens slowly over every second that you become consumed by them.

The way out is by knowing your worth, but if you never knew what that worth was or the potential that your life holds, you give it to anyone who shows a little bit of interest in loving you, fooling you into believing they have all the answers. I know it's hard to understand, because it is just as hard to explain it to you.

However, I was lucky enough to have people along the way to take off my blinders and shine a light in my face. I was one of the lucky ones who was woken up because those who did stick around shook me until I got it. I thank God every day for the blessings — even the bad ones — because without them I wouldn't be me and I sure as hell wouldn't be as strong as I am now.

What people don't realize is when a woman finds herself in an abusive and violent relationship, that relationship wasn't the first one that tore her down. Maybe it was the second, third, or seventh. It happens when horrible people begin to pick and pick at someone who is so trusting, yet doesn't know their true worth. I grew up thinking I wasn't tall enough, pretty enough, smart enough, thin enough, and most of all just not good enough, my entire life. When these so-called "men" came around and showed me attention and played on my emotions, I began to think, *Well, you're not good enough, so you better keep this one!* What a sad and lonely thought for a girl/woman to think of herself.

Those women and men who come before us, mothers, fathers, grandmothers, grandfathers, aunts, uncles, cousins, sisters, brothers, teachers, mentors, friends — they are the ones who are to teach the younger women that they are strong enough, pretty enough, smart enough, and most importantly, capable of anything because they are good enough just the way they are. Each woman has a uniqueness, a gift and a purpose to share with the world. A light that shall not be dimmed by anyone. If someone does try to dim that light and kill their fire, then others need to step in and protect them.

My abuser took all of my possibilities, and I got snuffed out like a fire in a hurricane.

However, the fire was inside me, deep inside me. What I thought I lost was pulled out of the ashes and brought back to life when I came home on that dreadful day I kicked him out.

It took everything I had, but my friend protected the little ember that I had remaining. It was my small sliver of strength and resilience that kept the fight in me. You see, I had no idea how the ember was ever going to come back to life, but it did, slowly. For that I am forever blessed.

AFTERTHOUGHT OF THE TIPPING POINT

When I was writing this chapter, I began with a naïve sense that I had only experienced a few incidents of abuse. As I continued writing my memoir, I quickly realized that was in fact not the case. From childhood to adulthood, I unfortunately have been abused emotionally, mentally, physically, and sexually. I recently had to discuss them with my therapist as I was placing blame on the one person who was innocent, me.

My very first memory of sexual assault is from my childhood was when I had to play the mom/wife in a game we called house. Not only was I young, I was always put in very uncomfortable situations. I thought that if I did what other kids said then maybe they would like me. These teenage boys would make me lie on them, expose themselves, and touch me. Though I had clothes on, it was still a violation. I didn't know my body was my body, what was mine was mine alone, and that no one could touch it without my permission. There were never any conversations about those things that I can recall.

Another time as a young girl, the neighbor boys in California would have me do things that seemed "not right," yet I was unaware that they were inappropriate.

While walking to school in eighth grade, I was harassed by a group of men who worked down the street from where I lived. They would hoot, holler, cat call, and say inappropriate comments as I walked by. I would make sure to cross the street before I got to that part of my walk home but it would still continue. No, there was not another direct route. Still frightened, I began walking about a half mile out of my way. Yet I didn't feel safe. I told my teacher, Mrs. Branson, and she didn't like it either. My dad worked, so she brought me home after school every day. I will always be thankful for her care and concern.

As a young woman I was sexually assaulted by a family member. I absolutely love back rubs (who doesn't?). I asked this family member to rub my back as they had done many times before. I didn't think anything of it, until this family member made me flip over and assaulted me by fondling my breasts. I was alone, frightened, and didn't know what to do. I listened to this person. I kept it to myself and never told anyone nor did I ever bring it up to this individual. I never put myself in a vulnerable situation with this person again. I have forgiven them.

My husband and I bought a house in 2016. I was in the process of putting in a professional gym where I now train my clients. I had gone to Home Depot to collect some paint swatches to see what colors I wanted to incorporate in my space. There were 10 feet between where I stood to the next closest thing behind me, which was the paint counter. All of a sudden, a man walked by as close to my backside as he could, grabbed my ass, and continued walking past me. I looked at him, he looked at me and said, "Oh, sorry about that!" I froze. I didn't know what to do. I was in shock. I gathered my paint swatches and went home.

I pushed it out of my mind in disbelief, like many of us women do. We are so conditioned to think that we were in the way, we did something wrong, or we "asked" for it, when in fact there are just *monsters* out there who think they can do whatever they want.

As the shock wore off, two days later I told my husband and he was furious. He was not mad at me, but he told me that I needed to report it. I did! I went to the police station and as I was shaking, I told the officer what happened and filed a report. I was given a case number.

The police officer took down the report, and told me he would follow up. I went to Home Depot and spoke to management. They wouldn't hand over the surveillance video to the police. I hired a lawyer to write a letter for all video footage to be released. Home Depot finally turned it over to the police, and the officer called me and told me to expect a follow up in seven days. I never heard from him. I followed up on several occasions. I had a client whose husband works for the police department and he looked into it. I was told the case doesn't exist. My husband and I have tried to get answers on multiple occasions! I was finally able to talk to someone and she informed me that in fact the case is in the system, it is still open, and she would have a Detective contact me. It has been three years; I still get anxious walking into a Home Depot and I can tell you I am on high alert every single time. People wonder why women don't report sexual assault. It's because it isn't taken seriously. Nothing seems to get done. However, that needs to change. We need to report *everything*. Then things will start to change.

Looking back and remembering all the times I was assaulted, I feel sad, beaten, and disgusted. Not with myself, but with those who thought it was OK to do such horrible things. Society says that it must be the woman's fault, she must have provoked it, asked for it and changed her mind, or she's a slut. Why don't we as a society stop pointing fingers at the victims and ask the perpetrators *why* they chose to abuse? This is where the conversation needs to start!

If we don't encourage women to speak up (as well as men who have also been abused), then we can't start the conversation, we can't bring awareness, and we can't implement change.

I hope by telling my story and speaking up and saying ***#metoo***, it will give others courage to do the same.

I am not to blame and neither are you! I will not tolerate such behavior from others anymore, nor should we as a society!

Chapter 4

Bodybuilding – My Days as a Figure Competitor

To be strong, you must first be weak. –Erin Baer

LESSON OF DISCIPLINE

Coach KP

I was just out of an abusive relationship, I was completely alone, and I didn't recognize myself. *Who had I become? Was this all life had for me, a broken and shattered soul who hated looking in the mirror every day?* I found myself numb to the core of my heart and left with pieces that I slowly started to pick up and gather.

I had no self-worth, no self-confidence, and no money. The monster took everything from me, or so I thought.

On April 1, 2009, I found myself in the midst of a court battle against my abuser, who had controlled everything. He hadn't let me talk to my friends and family. He had totally isolated me. I felt it was my fault. Why would they even accept me after all that? I had completely lost myself, my family, and my connection with God. I felt out of control and hated myself. I didn't know how I ended up in this place of confusion and self-hate. I certainly didn't like what I allowed myself to be put through in the past relationship and I didn't like my current reality. But as scary as it was to be alone, I knew it was by far healthier than the abuse I endured.

Sitting at my desk, I watched this stunning woman walk into the gym and into Coach KP's office. I found myself in awe. She was beautiful, fit, and had muscle. *Who was she, how did she get her body to look like that and how could I do the same?*

She walked right past me as if she was on a mission, into KP's office. I thought, *If I looked like that, no one would mess with me.*

Once Coach KP's door opened and she left, I marched myself right into his office and asked, "Who was that?" He told me that she was a figure competitor and top in the world. I went on asking him, "Wait, what's a figure competitor? As in, a woman who works out, gets on stage in a little, itty bitty sparkly bikini and lets people judge her?"

"Yup, that is exactly what she is!" he answered.

I soon found some hope that if someone like that existed, maybe there was hope for me yet. Maybe I could climb out of this deep, dark and lonely hole I found myself in — just maybe.

TAKING BACK CONTROL

My need for control was born on a Monday morning in the summer in 1997 in Princeton, Missouri when all I needed from my mother was a ride to golf camp.

I was attending a junior golf camp program that would take place every Monday for seven weeks. How exciting! I was one of two girls who attended the golf summer camp. I had a blast, and made the best of the lessons and rounds we were able to play. After all, I had huge goals and dreams when it came to my golf game. After our round in week six, the golf pro who oversaw the camps informed me that Nike was very interested in me and wanted to sponsor me the following summer. I just had to do one thing: show up on the last day of camp the following Monday. That was it. I was beaming from ear to ear, and when my mom picked me up, she thought it was wonderful . . . or so I thought.

Monday rolled around, I got dressed in golf attire, had my clubs, and I was ready to go. I went to my mom and told her I was ready and we needed to head out. She told me I wasn't going. I didn't know what she meant, so I asked for more explanation. She told me I wouldn't be going to camp. I was confused. I had a huge opportunity and all I had to do was show up, attend the last camp, and my following summer was set up for me with Nike!

She went on to tell me I was out of luck unless I could find a ride. I called my friend, but he was too busy to take me as he owned his own landscaping company. I asked and pleaded with my mom. I begged and begged. I didn't get to go. I was absolutely devastated, broken and let down. I couldn't believe it. Everything I had been working so hard for was about to pay off and I had no control to make it happen. None, zip, nada. I was heartbroken.

From that day forward, I learned a valuable lesson that I have held onto since. If I wanted to make sure I was never defeated, let down, or devastated, I needed to make sure I controlled absolutely everything. I have since sworn to myself that I would never be a failure unless I failed of my own accord.

After the abuse I felt shattered into a million pieces, and I was just trying not to crumble any further. I had finished graduate school a year prior, had no relationships or friendships, and hated myself. I was also in the midst of this court battle. I needed a goal and a positive distraction. Competing was the answer! It allowed me to focus and take back control of my own life, every single aspect. I walked into Coach KP's office and I said, "I want to compete!" He looked at me and said, "OK!"

It took six months of hard work along with sweat, blood and tears, but I did it. After my first show in October of 2009, I competed in my second show three weeks later. I placed in both shows and had four trophies to my name, but the emotional aftermath took a toll on me.

All the feelings I had pushed aside, buried deep down by lifting heavier weight, rep after rep, all came crashing down on my soul. It was a tidal wave of every emotion imaginable.

I competed in my second show with two other competitors of Coach KP's and they took first place and the overall competition in their classes. I took fourth and fifth place in my classes. I felt defeated.

When they say old habits die hard, they mean it. I immediately started slamming myself and putting myself down. Telling myself I wasn't good enough. I found myself in a war against myself and on both ends of the attack.

The competition was over. My goal had been accomplished, but I felt like a failure once again, more defeated than ever before. I had completely mind-fucked myself. I felt lost, alone, and thought I had disappointed my coach as well as myself.

I didn't know what to do.

Two women in the dressing room sat me down. They were blunt and matter-of-fact. One said, "Don't you dare, don't you dare speak about yourself that way!" The other, "You know what kind of guts it takes to do what you just did?"

They went on to tell me that I should be proud and not compare myself to others. That my only competition was myself. That was it! It takes a lot of self-discipline, hard work, and commitment to do what I did, they said. I should never make it about the trophy, but rather about myself and improving from show to show. They told me I needed to be kinder to myself and proud of my efforts. To know why I was doing this. They embraced me and went on to explain that my reasons for competing needed to be for *me* and no one else. And as soon as I didn't know my "why," I needed to hang up my suit and put the five-inch heels away.

Their words rang true and have stayed with me through the years.

Then I was in the midst of dealing with sickness after sickness, a court battle over domestic violence and sexual assault, going to both individual and group therapy and trying to control everything. I was just finding myself again, focusing on me and trying to move on from a world of pain, while pushing my limits physically as much as possible through bodybuilding. The emotional wreckage that consumed my mind, heart, and soul was a raging storm; no one needed to be a part of that.

Talk about not the perfect time to be getting into a relationship!

A good friend was on a dating site and encouraged me to get myself back out there. I hesitantly obliged and signed up. Sitting on my bed and creating a profile, I remember laughing the entire time.

After all, who wants this emotional mess as a partner? I was simply trying to make it one day at a time.

As I completed my profile, I decided to browse around. I clicked on a few profiles in the days that followed. I came across this picture of a man I thought was cute and kept on scrolling. Yup, I scrolled past the man I would spend hours looking for again, because that smile, I just couldn't shake it.

As I frantically searched for this man's profile picture, I found my thoughts consumed with craziness.

I finally found the picture, clicked on the profile (SexyMonkeyLoverer), and sent a message: "Hi, you have a nice smile." *How lame, I mean, what kind of message is that? Who would ever respond to a message that said you have a nice smile, ugh please?* I finally closed my laptop and went to bed.

To my pleasant surprise I got a response. However, when I read it, I was eye-rollingly disappointed. It sounded like Fonzie from *Happy Days*, when I read it. "How ya doin'?" *Seriously? How ya doin'? Oh goodness, what kind of guy is this?* Well, I decided to respond and we had our first official date on August 15, 2010, in downtown Denver. I drove around for an hour looking for a parking spot. Just as I wanted to give up, I pulled into a parking lot, closed my eyes briefly, told God that if this was meant to be, then there would be a parking spot. I opened my eyes and drove a little way down the street and there it was: an empty parking spot. Dressed in jeans and a pink and grey fitted T-shirt, I made my way to where he was waiting for me. I was nervous. *Please let this go well.*

Before this date, I had attempted to go on a couple other dates from the dating site and those were awful, awkward, and just not my style, not at all.

As I approached this man, I smiled, and as I went in for a handshake, he went in for a hug. *Oh no*, I thought. He asked if I was hungry. "Yes, of course!" After all, I was a bodybuilder, hello? He asked where I wanted to go and I picked the Cheesecake Factory, one of the most expensive restaurants I could think of. I knew *I* couldn't afford it.

Talk about being a little resentful toward men! I figured that if the date was going to be miserable, at least I would eat well. What a poor attitude to have. You have to remember, I had just gotten out of a terrible relationship 20 months earlier and didn't have many successful dates that summer.

After a late lunch we spent hours walking around, eating yummy food, and learning about one another. It was laid back once I got comfortable, but how badly can you screw up a first date? I surely thought I had.

Throughout our first date I called him a liar, didn't kiss him goodnight, and I hid behind a rock and ran to my car to avoid being seen by a creepy guy I knew. *Seriously, what kind of crazy was I?*

Once I got into my car and watched this wonderful man walk away, I immediately got on my flip phone and texted him. Yes, you read that right, not even 10 seconds from when I ninja-rolled myself into my car, I texted this guy. I assumed he thought I was absolutely nuts. I wrote to him that I had a great time and hoped to hear from him soon. He responded immediately. *Win!*

As you guessed, we started dating, I nicknamed him "Honey Baer," and the rest is history. We are happily married and he has played an enormous role in my successes from here on out.

After 2009 ended, 2010 came and went with many illnesses that prevented me from giving it my all in bodybuilding preparation. I decided in 2011 that I was more than ready to make another go at competing.

My court case wrapped up on August 23, 2010, and that chapter was closed. A new door was opened and a new year had just begun. I was ready. I had met a good man who knew all my secrets and still wanted to be with me. I was finally healthy again and ready for my next competition challenge. Ready to put on that itty bitty sparkly bikini and five-inch heels while being judged in front of hundreds. Now I just had to prep for it. I wasn't scared — I loved it. I was admittedly obsessed with bodybuilding. I had lost my control in the abusive relationship and all I wanted was to control everything. Competing gave me that. I began my prep for competition number three. It was exhilarating and hard.

I was criticized by so many people who just didn't understand the world I was living in. They accused me of starving myself, having an eating disorder, or doing dangerous things. I drowned out the naysayers and haters by doing more and more reps. I had a goal and nothing was going to stand in my way. I wasn't at all prepping in a dangerous way. I ate all the time, more calories and portions of food than I could count. I had a healthy and safe preparation, as my coach determined to make it so. Others were supportive and fascinated by it. They told me I inspired them. That fueled me more.

I had a desire to prove to the world and to myself that I could be knocked down but I wouldn't stay down. I would get up and I would fight. I was a fighter, and the bodybuilding stage was my arena. It gave me hope, and every time I stood on stage I felt that maybe the world and everyone in it would think I was good enough.

Coach KP was with me as my Coach from 2009-2012 and through four competitions. I placed in all of them and truly grew as a female competitor and a human being.

My Figure Competition stats with Coach KP are as follows:

2009

NPC VPX Carla Sanchez Fitness Fiesta

- Women's Open 5'2" – 5'4" – 4th place
- Women's Novice Figure Short Class – 5th place

NPC Axis Labs Colorado Open

- Women's Figure Novice Class A – 4th place
- Women's Figure Open Class B – 5th place

2011

NPC Max Muscle Mile High

- Novice Figure Class A – 2nd place
- Open Figure Class B – 4th place

2012

NPC Colorado Open

- Novice Figure Class A – 1st place
- Open Figure Class B – 1st place

He taught me the value of discipline and how I had that quality like no other. He taught me how one should never underestimate the underdog, and that those who go through hell are the ones who rise the highest. As I grew up, I was always underestimated; it is one quality I held onto that kept me motivated from a very young age. When people told me I couldn't or I wouldn't or I shouldn't, I always let that light my fire and I became even more focused. It is one thing that pushed me in school, golf and beyond. Coach KP grabbed onto that and taught me that I should just let people go ahead and underestimate me, judge me and tell me I can't, because we both knew it would only fuel my desire to be disciplined and catapult me into success in the bodybuilding arena.

I looked up to him as my coach, as a big brother and friend. He also underestimated me – one time, but never again. From that day forward he pushed me beyond limits I never even imagined as an athlete and as a person. He made me dig deep within myself to find my *whys*, and taught me to believe more in myself than anyone else, because at the end of the day it only matters how *you* feel when you see the person staring back in the mirror. He was right, and I will always be grateful for him seeing that potential in me, helping me hone in on true discipline, and teaching me to not let anything stand in my way if I so desired it.

Just as I was getting into a rhythm and liking who I was becoming, while taking back my control through bodybuilding, my life was turned upside down once again.

THE ACCIDENT

Mindfulness

Five years into my bodybuilding career, my life stopped on a dime and everything changed. I had four competitions under my belt, was newly married, and had just taken a job at a big box gym as a personal trainer. I went through the orientation process and finally had my first client. It happened to be Valentine's Day: February 14, 2013. This specific client had some previous injuries regarding her shoulder, so I wanted to make sure to pick the right exercises. I asked a colleague for some advice and felt confident for my first session. I was ready to go with her exercise plan in hand.

As I took my client over to the workout area of the gym, I explained to her what the one-hour session was going to look like and picked up a red resistance band with handles. I looped it around a 10-inch-wide metal rod that was about an inch thick. I proceeded to step back, stretching the resistance band with a handle in each hand. I then explained to my client that we would be doing external rotation. I started showing her the movement, starting with my elbows at a 90-degree angle, with the fingers of my fists facing the floor.

As I began to rotate my shoulders, allowing my gripped hands to raise towards the ceiling, I was struggling to get the movement right. I felt resistance, but it was not quite right. So I started again and BAM, I went to the floor, grabbing my forehead and falling to my knees.

I was confused and in severe pain. As soon as I pulled my hand away, blood was everywhere. I screamed; I had no idea what had just happened. Something had hit me hard and fast, right in the face.

I lay on the floor, covered in blood, blinded, surrounded by my coworkers. They used towel after towel to wipe the blood off my face and asked a million questions. I began sobbing in pain and trying to answer all the questions that were being thrown at me.

What the hell just happened? My head was pounding, blood was pouring out of my face like a leak in a busted pipe, and I was in extreme pain. It felt like mere seconds before the paramedics arrived, checking my vitals, asking me questions, wrapping my head in gauze bandages, and whisking me away in the snow on a gurney. As the doors of the gym opened, the snowflakes nipped my face. I shook from the cold, bitter air as it danced on my skin. They wheeled me into the ambulance and I was rushed off to the emergency room not knowing exactly what happened and what was under the blinding, bloody gauze that crowned my head.

When we arrived, my beloved husband was standing at the emergency doors. As I looked at him through my bloodstained tears, a look of terror was on his face — he was scared for me. All I could say was, "I'm sorry!" over and over again. And with a look of stricken grief he looked at me and said, "Don't be sorry, I just want you to be OK!"

I was wheeled back to the emergency room with my husband by my side. I couldn't see out of my left eye; my face began to swell and my head was pounding with horrible pain. The nurses started rushing around and assessing the damage.

Nurses took my vitals and asked me questions. The pain was becoming unbearable and my thoughts were scrambled as I myself was taking inventory of the horrible ordeal.

The doctor came in and began his examination. As he unwrapped my head, being careful and cautious, I sat still, scared of the horror underneath.

As he took off the final piece of the bandage, a rush of pressure began to surface, and my face swelled even more. I lay there dazed and numb from the shock.

As I cried, my tears burned not only my eyes but the flesh of my face like hot lava from a volcano. I wept as the doctor cleaned up the wound between my eyes. The doctor then began to stitch up my face, and he turned to my husband and told him how lucky I was to be alive. He proceeded to inform my husband, as if I weren't there, that if the rod that made contact with my face would have rotated another 90 degrees, it would have pierced through my skull, killing me instantly. (We found out later that the bar was not secure. When I pulled on the resistance band it pulled the bar out like a sling shot and nailed me right in the face between my eyes.) Here I was, covered in blood but lucky to be alive.

As the doctor finished off the sutures, I kept repeating that I couldn't open my left eye, that it was difficult to see, and that something was cutting it like a knife.

He kept insisting that everything was fine. But I knew it was far from fine. The emergency room is only equipped to do so much. That doctor diagnosed me with a double concussion and a traumatic brain injury (TBI). He discharged me from the emergency room several hours later and sent me directly to the eye doctor to be examined.

I was still covered in blood, which had dried along my hairline and face, separating the two like a river. My husband and I made our way up to the eye doctor.

Dizzy and in agony from the pain, I was led blindly to an exam room where the eye doctor would discover a 90 percent laceration of my left eye. He informed us that I might or might not get my vision back, and that he would like to see me in a week for a reexamination.

I couldn't process the information. I had just escaped with my life, my brain hurt, and I might lose my vision in my left eye. It was all very confusing. All I wanted to do was sleep, but I couldn't. My thoughts were disappearing as quickly as they entered my mind. It was all overwhelming.

The doctor prescribed antibiotics and steroid eye drops, which my husband would have to administer daily in hopes it would resolve the injury and prevent infection. The only thing I could do was rest and pray that my vision would be spared.

As my husband helped me cautiously to the car through the snowy parking lot, he held on to me tightly. My balance was not great and I couldn't see. He was my eyes.

I don't remember much of that life-changing day, but as night fell, he fed me French fries for dinner as I couldn't stomach anything else. I didn't want to eat, yet he insisted. I stayed in bed for what seemed like weeks, but in reality it was only a few days.

I couldn't see. I was instructed to keep my eyes closed. Even when I tried to open them, swelling from the injury caused too much pain.

I was finally able to get up and shower three days later. It was the best shower I had ever taken. As I washed my blood-filled hair, watching it run over my body into the drain, I closed my eyes. When I opened them, a rush of pain swallowed my left eye, the eye that was just beginning to heal. That day we found ourselves calling the doctor, explaining that I was taking a shower, and a dried-up scab of blood had found its way into my eye. The doctor said that my eye was vulnerable, and to prevent further damage I needed to wear an eye patch.

The next few weeks were filled with doctor visits and rest. No light, no TV, no sound, no reading, no screen time, just rest. Noise and light were a nuisance, but as stubborn as I was, I insisted the doctors let me go back to work. They should have never let me go back.

The complete diagnosis from the fluke yet horrific accident was as follows: double concussion as my brain crashed into the front and rear of my skull, along with short-term memory loss, a lacerated eye, possibly permanent eye damage, a traumatic brain injury, and many contusions and facial swelling.

I continued going to my primary doctor, but fought with worker's compensation insurance regarding the care and treatment I was currently receiving and the care that my husband and I knew I needed. He was more adamant than I, as I didn't realize the severity of my conditions.

I could remember the accident but I couldn't remember anything in the two weeks prior or what had happened seconds earlier. I was suffering from severe short-term memory loss.

My husband and I were watching a show and he made a reference to a movie we had watched two weeks prior to the accident (*Wreck-It Ralph*). I told him I had no idea what he was talking about or the actor he was referring to as I had never heard of him. The expression on my husband's face said it all. He stared at me blankly and began to tear up.

I was confused. *What did I say that was so sad, what had I done to make my husband cry?*

I asked him what was wrong. He explained to me that he was concerned for me and felt such a terrible sense of sadness because I looked so confused and didn't know what he was talking about.

I asked him to explain what he meant. He tried, but I couldn't even remember what he said seconds later, between one word and the next.

As soon as he realized the severity of the problem, he grew very patient with me through my recovery. This is not to say he wasn't patient before, but he definitely readjusted how he conducted conversations.

It became very frustrating for me. I began to realize I couldn't remember things; I couldn't remember the answers he would give me within seconds of the questions I asked. I just couldn't remember, so I would ask again.

I began getting angry at the world, angry at God, and mostly angry at myself because I had lost control once again and this time it was of my mind, my brain, the essence of me and my capabilities.

I was no longer able to control it. And I didn't know how to fix it.

It was a scary thing. As time went on it didn't seem to get better. We demanded that worker's compensation insurance get me the appropriate help. The brain has a small window of time in which it can heal and recover. This fact scared me. Even though my husband wouldn't share his thoughts about how it scared him until months later, he was frightened. I could see it written on his face.

After a lot of back and forth between worker's compensation and my doctor fighting for the care I needed, after a year, I was finally sent to the appropriate doctors. They began testing immediately, using brain scans and therapy to help me get the rehabilitation I needed.

It was a long and frustrating road. The bright red line between my eyebrows brought the truth of what had happened to my attention every time I had to bandage my face. Wearing a large eye patch made it worse. It was like a white letter across my forehead that welcomed stares, laughs, confusion and questions from everyone I passed. Whispers began to fill the void in the silence at work, and those around me began pointing and making fun of what had happened. I was beyond self-conscious. It didn't help when a pastor from a local church looked at me and said, "At least I don't have a hole in my face!"

I was soon diagnosed with post-concussion syndrome (PCS) and post-traumatic stress disorder (PTSD), and had to seek help to deal with the realities of my accident. It was difficult and most exasperating, especially when people I thought cared would make the statement: "Just get over it!" Here I was struggling with my appearance, the limitations I now had since the accident, and learning how to cope with my diagnoses and memory loss, and people were telling me to just get over it.

I began secluding myself, judging myself, and hating myself because I didn't recognize who I was. I couldn't work out, I couldn't cover my face with makeup because of possible infections, and I couldn't pretend it had never happened. I couldn't hide it, as much as I tried.

The worst part of the entire situation was my memory. As time slowly went on I began to understand the severity of it all. How bad my memory was and how long the road to recovery would be. My life hasn't been the same since that terrible accident. I still have moments of memory loss, problems with overstimulation, and when I bump my head, I have major PTSD.

Once you become conscious of your own mind's shortcomings, it is a scary reality. I would have good moments and then be flooded with really bad ones.

The PTSD and frustrations from the accident got so bad that I had to seek psychological therapy and rehabilitation. I felt alone once again as no one understood the depth of my worries and the fears that lay in my heart.

I began seeing a therapist who specialized in biofeedback. Biofeedback is an incredible technique that helped me gain greater awareness of my body, the way it would react, and how I could manipulate it with my breath and concentration to a response that worked for me. I became aware of how my body would respond to fear, stress, anxiety, depression and overstimulation. From there I harnessed the techniques and was able to reduce my heart rate, muscle contraction, sweat gland response, breath, and temperature, and become more mindful. Patience, which I hated, was becoming my reality.

To the average person this may not seem like much, but it changed my world. With biofeedback, the idea is to get the two major subdivisions of the autonomic nervous system to be in sync with one another. The two are the sympathetic nervous system, which is our involuntary processes that speed up bodily processes, and the parasympathetic nervous system, which consists of the involuntary processes that slow down bodily processes. All I needed to know was how I could get back to controlling something in my life again, and it started with my mind.

Most people, when charted, were within a certain range and could confidently get their systems to work well together. When my doctor pulled my chart to see how well I could control my autonomic system, she was speechless, as my results were literally off the chart. I was shocked. I first thought maybe I had failed, but it was quite the opposite. I was so in tune with my body that I was off the charts by tens of thousands. I felt like a superstar. I had started gaining some control back and it opened a gate to hope I thought I had lost.

This was when I realized that when I focused, I could control myself and how I react to something. It just takes practice, confidence, and focus.

My world was no longer how I remembered it. I had to adapt to my new reality with a TBI that would take time to heal, and a memory that was unreliable.

After returning to work, I endured five more head injuries, all fluke accidents. The injuries kept pushing me backwards, and I had not completely healed from that dreadful day in February 2013. My eye has healed beautifully, and my vision is perfect, thank God! I still have memory issues, and I am more prone to concussions. What lies ahead for me as I grow old, frightens me. However, I work on my healing every day and sometimes I forget how far I have come. I just have to remember that I have overcome so much in my life up to this point. My brain injury wasn't the end of me, not yet anyway.

A note on healing: Every year after my heart condition diagnosis, I went in for a checkup. Every year until 2015, that is. My checkup that year showed that my heart condition was cured! The doctor told me that I no longer had to say that I had it. He could not explain this miraculous healing, but I give credit to my years of exercise and healthy diet, and to the strength and control I gained through biofeedback. Regardless of how it happened, I consider it a miracle!

LESSON OF PERSISTENCE

Coach LeAnn

I was preparing for my fifth competition with Coach KP, but he was at a different point in his life and it seemed he was drifting away from the competition world. While we are still friends and I will always be grateful for his guidance, at the time I felt left behind. Abandoned once again. It was only eight weeks before the show, and I knew I didn't look like I was eight weeks away, but rather three months. I felt insecure and unprepared. It was a new and frightening feeling. I had a conversation with one of the competition judges I had developed a friendship with.

My friend told me about Coach LeAnn. She was not only a coach but had competed herself, and was also a judge in Colorado. I was desperate and needed a second pair of eyes on my physique.

I canceled my appointment with my former coach and met with Coach LeAnn. At one point, she made a statement that we both laugh about to this day. As she was analyzing my physique she said, "I know that waist! I have seen it before!" I thought maybe she had judged me in a show, but that wasn't it. She pulled out her phone and asked me what shows I had done. I told her. She brought up her competition photos. That was it! She and I had competed in a show against one another several years prior. It was my second show, her first show, and I beat her by two points. Oh, we laughed. I had beaten her and now she was my coach. The irony.

She finished looking at my physique and then told me straight up that the next eight weeks were going to be hell, but as long as I was persistent and didn't miss a beat it would all be worth it! I was not sure if I was ready, but I also hated failing or giving up. I was all in and so was she! I put all my trust in her — I had to if I was going to get the work done.

She wasn't wrong when she told me to expect hell. The next eight weeks were intense and brutal. I cried, I sweated, I pushed through pain and beyond any limit I could ever imagine. I was sore every day, yet more determined than I had ever been. I was not about to let my coach down, let alone myself. I worked harder than I had ever worked before. I saw her weekly for check-ins. When I wasn't directly in front of her I was sending her pictures every morning of my physique, the details of my workout, and telling her about every bite I took and every ounce of water I drank. I was in constant contact with my coach. If there was an hour that went by, she was texting me, asking how things were going. During our weekly check-ins, she would work me out so hard, that sometimes I felt I couldn't lift another weight. She pushed me. She believed in me. I was determined to not take the eight weeks for granted. I was hyper focused and dedicated to bringing a better package to the stage. Only eight weeks to do the work, a challenge that seemed impossible, yet I buckled down anyway.

I did everything she said to perfection.

The day of competition I stepped on stage knowing I had given it my all. I brought what I thought was my best package to date. She was right there with me.

As prejudging started, she sat in the audience cheering me on, instructing me to do whatever it was to make myself stand out to the judges. We did our individual routines and then lined up at center stage for comparisons by doing our quarter turns. I did mine with ease and was in the pose before any other girl. It gave me an advantage; the judges would see me first and for a longer time. I stood confident and fierce, as if I walked and posed like this naturally. I had put hundreds of hours in to make it look so effortless.

That night during finals, there was nothing more I could do except walk on stage, line up, and wait. Wait to see if my eight weeks of hell paid off.

As I waited, listening for my number to be called out, I knew this time was different. It showed me that just putting myself out there was the reward! Smiling, standing in model pose as the head judge began his call outs, I knew that my persistence and determination was about to pay off.

I placed second in my Open Class B in the NPC Max Muscle Mile High in May of 2014. I was over the moon that I had pulled it off. Yet I knew I could do better and I found my drive once more.

As soon as I took my suit off and slipped my feet out of my five-inch clear heels, my coach and I were planning our next prep. I thought it wouldn't be until 2015, but I was wrong. It would be much sooner.

My coach believed in me so much. She thought I needed a bigger challenge and to compete in a larger show. She suggested the Rocky! *The Rocky? Was she crazy?* As I looked at her, wide-eyed, I gulped. I couldn't believe she had just said the Rocky. *Eek.* I had sworn years earlier that I would never compete in The Rocky. It was a huge show; it intimidated the shit out of me.

Well, that is when I learned to really never say never.

I trusted her! We went for it. We prepped for six months and our main goal was, as always, to bring a better package than the last show.

Each competition is completely different. You never know what is going to happen, who is going to show up, what the judges will be looking for, or how big your class is until the day of the show.

I was in control of everything leading up to competition day. What I ate, when I worked out, how hard I worked out, how much water I drank, when and if I posed, and my attitude. Once you step on stage all you can do is present your best package by posing and smiling. Stage presence is everything, and I perfected it!

I did compete in the Rocky and I did well in a stacked competition. I ended up placing second place in my Open Figure Class B. But I wanted more.

After the Rocky, my coach and I formed a dream together. We wanted to take Colorado and dominate it. I was well on my way. With six competitions under my belt, I was recognized by the judges and competitors. I knew I had what it took to make my dream into a reality.

I had taken first place before and I knew I could do it again. I had always told myself I would level up and compete nationally if and only if I competed, placed first in my class, and then took the overall championship title. Until then, I wouldn't waste my time.

I had already been in prep mode since the beginning of 2014 and had competed in two shows that year. So extending my prep and perfecting my physique only made sense. I was on track and I wanted to stay there, so I did.

We got to work one week after the Rocky. Our focus was to bring a completely better package that was undeniably overall champion material. One the judges couldn't ignore.

I worked tirelessly day in and day out. Spending hours in the gym, drinking gallons of water, and eating more food than I could fathom. I did whatever I had to stay one step ahead of my competition. Outworking them in all ways necessary.

My prep for the next competition was no small task. It was a full-time job.

I met with Coach LeAnn once every few weeks for check-ins and workouts. As the competition drew closer our visits became more frequent.

We changed everything about me. We perfected my physique, designed a new suit, and changed my hair from a deep brown to a golden brown blonde.

Finally, check-in night for the competition arrived. I was unrecognizable. No one realized it was me, Erin Baer, checking in. I shocked everyone, as we had kept the fact that I was competing a little secret as the show was drawing closer. I stayed off social media to avoid all mind fucks.

We wanted the shock factor.

The judges knew me and my competition feared me. I was a force to be reckoned with and we all knew it. I worked harder than anyone.

I stayed completely covered during the check-ins. I wanted everyone to wonder what was underneath the big, baggy clothes that covered my physique.

I got my three coats of spray tan, practicing my poses as I calmed my mind. When I was dry and a shade of Oompa Loompa, I made my way down to check in and picked up my number for the competition.

I had a feeling this was my time.

Competition day arrived. Staying covered, I got my makeup done professionally. As my coach and I did my hair, she kept me calm through stories, chatting about everyday life, and laughs. Finally, it was time to get in my suit and get my final spray tan as well as glue my bottom piece down. You don't want any suit malfunctions on stage.

I looked amazing. Everything was perfect. My hair, my makeup, and my attitude.

I ate my yams and boiled ground turkey, keeping my physique covered as we waited for my class to be called.

Finally, it was getting closer to prejudging, so we headed backstage to get me uncovered, oiled up, and pumping up for the stage while also going through my poses one last time.

I was ready. I could sense the fear from my competitors as their eyes followed my every move. I walked past and took my place in line. It was go time.

I turned my smile on, stood tall and stepped on stage. I did my individual routine, and got back in line. I had nailed it flawlessly.

Time for comparisons. They lined us all up, and we did our quarter turns as instructed. The judges started moving us around by calling out the numbers that were pinned on our left hips and switching us to other spots. They needed to get better views. We did our quarter turns again and again as they continued to place us in different spots within the lineup. Finally, they placed me in the center. This was a good thing, but not a guarantee. We were guided through two more rounds of quarter turns and then we were led off stage. The prejudging portion was over.

Now I had to wait five long, grueling hours. I made the most of it. I lay on the floor clothed, as my back was killing me at the time. I ate my food, drank small sips of water, chatted with my husband, checked in with my coach, and rested with my feet up while I listened to music. Five hours went by quickly. Before I knew it, finals had arrived.

I began touching up my hair and getting my tan rolled out one last time before I had to hit the stage to hear the results.

All I could think of was the hard work, sweat, tears, the relentless persistence that my coach instilled in me during my prep, and how proud I was of myself. How thankful I was for my coach. She never once abandoned me.

I took the stage, lining up on the side diagonal stage right after one last time for each of our individual routines. We were taken off the stage, waiting behind the curtain. We waited in hopes of hearing our number called as one of the top five.

One by one, the numbers of other girls were called to the stage. Two spots were taken, then a third, then my number; I had made the top five. I was overjoyed.

The placing began.

"In fifth place… In fourth place…" I was still standing stage right; my number had not been called. I realized I was now in the top three, already qualifying for nationals. The judge proceeded, "In third place…" OK, I am ecstatic. I'm in the top two. I actually have a chance to win this thing. "In second place…" *Oh my gosh, is this happening? Did I win my class?* The judge went on, "And our first place in Figure Open Class A is number 70, Erin Baer!"

I did it! I had won my class!

I stood tall, proud and in disbelief. I was beyond thrilled. A rush of emotions flooded my heart.

I couldn't get too excited just yet. There was one last thing to do: compete for the Overall Champion title within Figure Open at the NPC Natural Colorado. I had to deliver my physique one more time.

As the show went on, I waited for the other Figure Classes to be judged. Winners were announced, and my coach gave me instructions to gulp down some raw honey to get my blood to fill my muscles one more time.

It was time to take the stage once more, this time against all Figure Open Class winners. I was competing for the Overall Champion title.

As we did our quarter turns, I kept my smile on the entire time, even during the back pose. I was on fire! I owned every turn. As we stood in our model poses, we waited for what seemed like forever. A judge with a small white piece of paper walked over and handed it to the MC of the show. I held my breath with every muscle flexed. The MC began to speak. "Your 2015 NPC Supplement Natural Colorado Open Figure Overall Champion is Class A, Erin Baer!"

I did it, I really did it.

I won the overall!

My dreams had become a reality. As the trophy was placed at my feet, the other class winners and I grabbed hands and threw our arms in the air in victory. The photographer took a few photos and my competitors left the stage. I stayed there front and center with the trophy at my feet and struck my model pose for a picture. I smiled, beaming with joy and knowing I could now prep for a national show.

Coach LeAnn was waiting for me backstage and her expression said it all! She was proud. Proud of me, and most of all proud of our teamwork. It wasn't just me that won that day; we both won. I couldn't have done it without her. She kept pushing me beyond what I thought I could do. She taught me how to be persistent. Without that lesson I don't know if I would have succeeded as well as I did that day.

The work wasn't over. We had our eyes on a national show and a chance of earning my Pro Card, which designates a professional bodybuilder, one of the best in the nation.

We decided to prep for Junior Nationals in Chicago, in June 2016. I worked even harder than I had for the previous show. Coach LeAnn was able to secure me a sponsorship and have the entire prep and competition paid for. My sponsor was Bill Romanowski (yes, the retired professional football player). The prep was the most difficult prep I had ever endured.

As my eighth competition drew closer, I worked harder. I was focused and I had my goal in sight. My coach and I flew to Chicago and we checked in. Weighing 105 pounds and at 4 percent body fat, I was ready. This would be my best physique to date and the leanest I had ever been. The Junior National competition was held over a two-day period, with prejudging one day and finals the next. I did everything perfectly from start to finish, from prep to stage. I competed against 15 other women that day. I missed the top 10 by one and did not achieve professional status.

It was intimidating as my competitors were much taller and bigger than I am. Yet, I was proud. I had made it to the national level and competed against the best of the best. During the prejudging round I could tell the head judge wanted to pick me; I had a perfect physique. She kept making eye contact with me and pointing, whispering in the ear of the judge next to her. They had to make a hard decision. I understand and I am not mad or bitter about it at all. Bodybuilding is a complicated sport. Many get involved with intense supplements and when you're in that world you can tell those who are and those who are not. The women I went up against were beasts. I was jacked, with a waist that measured 18 inches. I fit all the criteria the judges wanted; I was just smaller in comparison.

After Junior Nationals, I was disappointed and figured, *I had a good run.* But as the weeks passed, I thought, *The hell am I done!* I decided I wanted to compete again.

My Figure Competition stats with Coach LeAnn are as follows:

2014

NPC Max Muscle

- Open Figure Class B –2nd place

NPC METRx Rocky

- Open Figure Class B –2nd place

2015

NPC Supplement Giant Natural Colorado

- Open Figure Class A –1st place
- Open Figure Overall Champion

2016

NPC Jr. USA

- Placed 11th out of 16

I had just finished running a local golf tournament for the World Amateur Golfers Tour. I couldn't believe how much fun I was having being back in the golf world again after taking a break for several years. I had a blast; I was respected and I was back to my number one passion: golf.

I had forgotten how good it felt to hit a little white ball into a little hole, 2 ¼ inches in diameter to be exact. On my way home, my phone rang and it was someone I thought was a friend, let's call him JW. JW was known in the bodybuilding industry because he had a nutritional and apparel company that would sponsor athletes (I was not one of them).

He wanted to talk about my career as a figure competitor and asked me what my next plans were. I told him, "LeAnn and I are going to work really hard and go for my pro card next year and earn it!" He responded, "That's great, but it won't happen unless you do what you're doing for five years or more."

I was shocked as I responded, "Well, I don't have five years as I would like to have kids someday and I am not getting any younger."

JW's response was, "It won't happen unless you do injectables, and even then you may not earn your pro card!"

At this point, I was upset but I held my tears as I responded, "I am not doing injectables. I want to have kids and I guess I just may have to call it quits." I was devastated.

This person, this influencer in the industry was supposed to be a friend and supporter, and here he was popping my balloon, telling me I didn't have a chance in hell in earning my pro card as a figure competitor in the world of bodybuilding.

What was I to do? I loved competing, but I wasn't about to do injectable steroids. I wanted a family with my husband, I wanted to have a healthy and long life, and I had a dream of earning my pro card. I had a decision to make. *Keep doing what I am doing or turn to the dark side?* I texted my coach immediately and we talked. I mulled it over for two days, and on September 28, 2016, I decided to retire from competing.

I knew right then and there my dream of being a professional figure competitor was over and my dream of being a mother and having a family of my own was about to start.

Chapter 5

The Infertility Journey

Believe, believe in something even if it seems impossible. –Erin Baer

As a little girl, I had dreams, big dreams and plans! In my father's eyes I was a princess and could conquer the world, but to everyone else I was a skinny, stupid, good-for-nothing girl. I was out to show my family, my non-existent friends, and everyone in between that I was better than they could ever imagine, and I set out on a journey to prove everyone wrong!

I had many dreams and aspirations growing up. I *was* going to be a princess, an astronaut, a scientist, a professional golfer; I would become famous and I was going to DINK it (dual income, no kids). I sure wasn't going to have the house on the hill, with a white picket fence, two dogs and 2.5 kids! *Are you out of your mind?*

No way! People didn't like *me*, so why in the world would I bring kids into the world and have them experience what I went through? However, I had my mind set on getting married, both of us climbing up the corporate ladder and living a financially secure life, traveling in the summers and growing old together.

Well, life is funny and as a believer in God, well, he has his own sense of humor when it comes to our plans. At least for me.

I didn't date until I was in college, and I certainly didn't pick the best guys for the job. Failed relationship after failed relationship convinced me that kids just weren't in the picture for me. I couldn't even find a guy who loved me. How in the world was I going to find a man to marry me, let alone have children with?

Well, my idea of DINKing it and not having kids all changed the moment Zach and I became an item, then engaged, and then married.

I was 34 and my husband was 37 and we figured, let's make sure we are in good health before we "pull the goalie" and get pregnant. I had this idea that because I was "young" (advanced maternal age is 35) that I was going to get pregnant the first month, while my husband was hoping for a full six months of fun!

I went to my gynecologist and had a blood panel done, a pap smear and an overall physical. While my husband procrastinated about going to the doctor, it didn't stop us once we got the OK to make a baby.

I went to my chiropractor weekly to make sure I was in alignment, I started on prenatal supplements, I kept up on my healthy eating habits and tracked everything — I mean everything. The first month went by and my period showed up. I was disappointed, but it was only the first month. After all, we had done everything we could to prevent pregnancy for the past six years and now we weren't. Let me tell you, it's a whole new game.

One month turned into two, and two turned into three. Then we were at the dreaded six-month mark. All the books say if you're in your 30s and haven't conceived in six months, seek help. Well, my doctor said the same thing.

As the six months came and went, I begged my husband to go get his swimmers analyzed. He kept putting it off.

Then one day, he said to me, "I scheduled an appointment!"

Honestly, I had no idea what he was talking about. I had given up trying to convince him that he needed to get tested to make sure our not getting pregnant wasn't his doing. When he told me he had made an appointment, I wasn't following.

I asked him for clarification and he told me, "I found a fertility clinic that is covered under our insurance and they are doing a special this month where I can get my swimmers analyzed for free!" He was so excited. He told me that I was going to be impressed, as he refers to his swimmers as "Super

Sperm." As the results did show, he does have super sperm.

If it wasn't him, that meant it must be me. But I was healthy, I ate right, I exercised every day, I got my sleep, I brushed my teeth . . . the list in my head went on and on and on. I was so confused.

Maybe it *was* me and there was something seriously wrong.

As a woman who wants nothing more than to be a mom, making that phone call to the fertility clinic is one of the hardest phone calls to make, in my opinion.

Zach and I went in for a consultation to discuss his results in more detail and for me to get my tests started. I was scared and confused, but all in all I was hopeful that we just needed to figure out what was going on and what we needed to do to make our dreams of being a family a reality.

We went over Zach's numbers and then they hauled me off to a different room to begin my testing right away. It was very reassuring and frightening all at the same time.

They did everything — weight, height, blood pressure, blood work, and an ultrasound. They then scheduled our follow-up appointment with our fertility doctor for eight weeks later. I called these the dreaded eight weeks, as I just wanted to know what was going on and what we needed to do!

The day finally came to meet with the fertility doctor. He was going to tell us what was next. If you've been where I have been, you know the way the doctor's office looks. It's like you see in the movies: one large, fancy desk; a big office chair; and on the other side, where the patients sit, two large leather chairs. Hanging where you can see them are the doctor's credentials, and of course, don't forget about the plant in the room and the neutral color paint on the walls, and a window with a view. Yes, this was the office in which we were about to hear my results and what they showed. How intimidating, exciting, and anxiety-producing all at the same time!

"First, I want to just say, there is nothing bad in this report." Those were the words that came out of the doctor's mouth. I couldn't comprehend, and I asked for clarification. He informed us that nothing in my blood work, tests, or ultrasounds showed any reason for infertility, which meant it was *unexplained.*

"Unexplained?" I asked. "You mean to tell me I am a healthy, 35-year-old female and we don't know why I can't get pregnant?"

"That's right," he answered.

I looked at my husband in disbelief.

It's one of those moments when you're relieved there is nothing wrong with you, but then you wish you had an explanation. At this point, we had unsuccessfully been trying to conceive naturally for the past 18 months; it hadn't worked and now we learned that both of our numbers looked great. *We look great on paper, so now what?*

Because I had reached "advanced maternal age" and we hadn't conceived naturally, even though we had no issues that suggested infertility, we were defined as "unexplained infertility" and needing medical intervention.

We were completely stunned and wanting to know the next steps. The doctor explained we had two choices: IUI or IVF! *What?* Here is the start to learning new vocabulary on top of trying to get pregnant.

Let me explain, just as the doctor did to us. Both options require the woman to take fertility medications. IUI stands for intrauterine insemination, which essentially means they do your husband's part for him. That's right, he gets to go into a room and enjoy himself to get those swimmers out, while I wait.

Once complete, he and I wait for about a half hour, while they check his sample, wash it and get it ready. After that, they take us into a room and it's my turn.

Our other option was IVF, which stands for in vitro insemination. That, my friend, is what used to be called the test tube baby – how literal! The woman's eggs are harvested under anesthesia. Once they have the eggs, hubby gets to have fun again and provide a fresh sample if frozen isn't being used. A sperm is then planted into an egg and becomes fertilized. The doctors then wait five days and implant the fertilized egg in hopes it takes. After a certain period of time, it's surgery for the woman.

After our doctor had explained our two options, he led us into a room so we could discuss our options as a couple and make a choice.

I knew what I wanted to do, and hubby knew what he wanted to do. We told the doctor that IUI was covered by insurance, while IVF was not, so if we did pick an option it would be IUI.

No-brainer, right? Wrong. We left the office angry at the whole situation. Neither one of us could understand why we had unexplained infertility and were given only two options. I wanted to proceed with IUI and hubby wanted to have one more month of natural baby dance.

We argued for two days, until I talked to a doctor friend who provided a middle-ground solution. Amen.

My friend suggested we do a cycle with the good parts of each. I asked for more clarification to make sure I understood what she was saying. "Well, your husband wants to try one more month naturally and you want the medical assistance, right?"

I answered with an upset, "Yes."

She responded, "Then do both. You take the medicine you need and then do timed intercourse." I couldn't believe I hadn't thought of that; I was so wrapped up in getting what I wanted that I wasn't looking at all our options. I immediately hung up with her, called my husband and asked if he would be OK with that? He was!

I called the fertility clinic right away and we got started that day. I went in, got my blood work and ultrasound done and started on letrozole to prepare for my day 12 ultrasound, and then day 14-16 fertilization the old-fashioned way. It failed. New month, new try.

It was July 2018, and we decided to start down the road of a medicated IUI cycle. We were nervous, anxious, excited, scared, and happy all at that same time. This was a new path and it wasn't guaranteed, but it was better than the odds stacked against us.

During the process of working with a fertility clinic, everything is based off the woman's cycle. Talk about getting over the "Too Much Information" (TMI) and just telling it how it is.

My period was officially here and I had to call the clinic to begin my IUI cycle. "Hi, this Erin Baer, I am on day one of my cycle."

They responded, "OK, great, can you come in on day three, before 10:30 a.m. for your blood work and ultrasound?" *Like I have a choice at this point.*

"Yup, I'll be there!" I responded.

How nerve-wrecking, was this really happening? Our first medicated cycle with assisted baby dancing was under way, our first IUI. *Would this work? What if it does and what if it doesn't? Will we actually be parents as we had hoped? Will it hurt? Will I be able to do the two-week wait with patience? Do I tell anyone what we're doing? What if I do, will it jinx it?*

So many questions that I kept asking myself. I found it soothing. Asking questions was my way to pray without praying.

We went in for our IUI on a Sunday morning. Saying I was scared and excited is a huge understatement of all the emotions I was experiencing. The nurse went over the procedure and told me to get undressed from the waist down. I was shaking like a leaf, filled with emotions, and freezing in that small room. With my husband by my side and his hand in mine, the nurse began. It starts out like a pap smear, so not too bad. Then the pain started — the agony was horrendous. *Is this really happening?* I was hoping for smooth sailing. I was wrong.

It was the longest two minutes of my life. The nurse finished the IUI and lifted the table so that my hips would be at a 45-degree angle. I was to lie there for 15 minutes. I immediately began to feel sick. Extremely sick! I thought I was going to vomit, pee and poo myself while passing out all at the same time. Those 15 minutes lying there with my hips tilted and my knees bent were torturous. Finally, the sweet ring of the timer went off and my husband helped me up. I got dressed and immediately asked the nurse if what I was feeling was normal? She looked confused and I then excused myself to the restroom where I remained with dizziness for the next 10 minutes.

I was given ginger ale and some crackers for the ride home. It took about an hour and a half before I started feeling normal. Good thing, as I had a golf lesson to give and clients to train later that day. The day passed and my week began. But thank God we had a distraction — my older brother Tyler's wedding down in Texas.

That Thursday, my husband and I went to Texas to be reunited with family and celebrate my brother's matrimony to his beautiful bride.

We enjoyed being in the sun, swimming, and eating all kinds of food, especially Whataburger (Zach's favorite). It was a great distraction, but at the end of each day the question of pregnancy would weigh on my mind again. I did my best to keep the question on hold.

The two-week wait was finally over and test day was here. The at-home test was negative. I tested the next day and it was negative. I convinced myself that it was OK and maybe we'd have better luck next time. After all, it was only the first try with an IUI cycle. *I mean, how lucky would that be?*

A couple of days passed and my period hadn't come. I was confused. I decided that I should test again just to calm my nerves and to be certain that my period was on its way. I took the test; I was sure it was going to be negative and tossed it on the shelf in the bathroom.

I kept myself occupied for a few minutes and decided it would be best to check the test so I could go about my day. I was a bit annoyed that I even thought I had to do another test after two failed ones in the days before.

I picked up the test, glanced at it, and then glanced again and gasped. *Wait, this can't be!* Day 17 after the IUI and it was *positive*! I started to shake, immediately ran into my husband's office and told him we were *pregnant*!

He looked at me with shock and excitement in his eyes as well as disbelief. He asked me how I knew and I told him I had taken another test and two pink lines appeared. I showed him. I asked him to read the box and to make certain he saw two lines as well. He confirmed. We embraced and I ran downstairs, as I had a client waiting for me. I was gleaming, with a huge smile on my face. I just couldn't hold it in. She was like family anyway, so I told her, "I'm pregnant!" I immediately called the fertility clinic and was seen that day to confirm that I was expecting.

What a wonderful day! Finally, we were expecting and I just couldn't believe it. I scheduled my ultrasound for September 6, 2018, when we would get to see our little one and hear the heartbeat. The weeks couldn't fly by quickly enough!

My husband and I went to the bookstore where he took some silly videos of me, and we found and bought the books we felt were best! What a joyous day!

I told the people who needed to know: my chiropractor, massage therapist, and some clients who to me were family. I began craving cucumbers and cream cheese. I would make a wrap every day filled with that along with tomatoes and spinach. They were delicious. My pregnancy symptoms started soon after we tested positive for a bun in the oven. My breasts were so tender that I hated not wearing a sports bra and when I showered, I didn't dare let the water hit them as the pain was terrible.

The days and weeks began to pass and my husband and I began counting down the days until our first ultrasound, where the pregnancy would become a reality.

September 4 rolled around and I didn't feel quite right. My beautiful cat, Gwendolyn, was on my stomach while I sat in my chair. She was acting odd and I just figured that she knew I didn't feel well. I felt like my period was coming, but that couldn't be . . . as I was pregnant.

I had to use the bathroom and when I wiped, there was a little bit of light blood. I excused it as no big deal. As the day went on, more blood began to appear. I called the fertility clinic and they assured me it would all be all right, that I would hear that heartbeat in a couple of days and my worries would be laid to rest. However, as the day drew to a close and we were supposed to go to a concert that night, the blood had darkened, thickened, and clotted. Something was seriously wrong. I told my husband that I didn't feel well, I was bleeding, and something was not right. I began to notice that all my pregnancy symptoms were disappearing, and I began to weep. I know my body better than anyone; I know when something isn't right. Something was going terribly wrong. That night I called the clinic again and they assured me I would be OK. But I wasn't.

The next day, as the bleeding began to get heavier and heavier, cramps and discomfort soon followed. I called again and the clinic just told me to wait for my appointment on September 6. I was devastated. I knew I was losing the baby and I couldn't do anything to stop it. I kept my husband up to date and he insisted that this couldn't be happening. He hoped maybe we were pregnant with two and we were only losing one. I knew it was bad and I felt horrible because of the pain my husband would soon experience when he realized our reality of pregnancy and expecting were over.

I went to bed that night in hopes that the bleeding would stop and all would be OK in the world, but I knew it was unlikely. I was devastated and broken. I began to pray and ask God, *Why would this happen? What did I do wrong? Did I work out too hard? Did I not eat enough food? Drink enough water?*

The next morning arrived and I woke up empty. I got ready for the day, put a smile on my face, trained my clients, and anxiously waited for my appointment. An appointment that I had previously been so excited for, I was now dreading. *Could we just rewind time by a few days?*

I didn't want to go to the appointment, but I had to because I knew putting it off wasn't an option, nor would it change anything that was happening.

My husband and I headed off to the appointment that afternoon. With tear-filled eyes, I walked into the clinic and was greeted by the receptionist as I signed in with an upbeat, "Hi, how are you?" I responded tearfully with, "Horrible." I just knew that I was losing my baby and it would soon be confirmed.

We waited. The ultrasound tech called me back with sympathy in her voice and led me to the ultrasound room. I explained to her that I was certain I was miscarrying. Walking in the room was heart-wrenching, because weeks before it was in preparation for a baby. It felt like déjà vu, only this time instead of seeing a baby, I was certain I was losing one. She instructed me to get undressed from the waist down and to get on the table.

As she inserted the cold, hard plastic wand, I took a deep breath as I watched her facial expressions and her deep concentration. Her facial lines softened and her eyes deepened with sorrow, and at that moment I could tell it wasn't good. I asked her cautiously with a careful slowness in my voice, "Can you see anything, anything at all?"

As she turned and looked at me with an empathetic expression in the contours of her face, I held my husband's hand, squeezing it tighter as I heard the words slowly form as she spoke. "I just see a lot of blood, I am so sorry!"

I wept as I turned my head towards my husband, feeling my heart break. She continued the exam carefully, to not cause me any (more) pain. When she was finished, she politely asked me to get dressed and said she would have me meet with the nurse to discuss the next steps. My world felt as if it ended right there in that room as I saw my husband's heart break along with mine.

I slowly got dressed, hugged my husband, and expressed my apologies with sorrow and sympathy for him . . . for us. As we were led into a consultation room, my mind began to race and my emotions stormed within my broken heart. How could this be happening? I became angry with the faith I had put in God. I didn't find comfort in my thoughts as they twirled in my mind. My emotions whirred as we waited until finally our nurse arrived. We knew it wasn't good, but nothing could have prepared us for the news we were about to receive.

As our nurse expressed her condolences for our loss, the room emptied and I felt as if I was in a white tunnel that was filled with deep pain. As I came to the surface of my sorrowful river, a rush of waves consumed me as the news that followed made it even more frightening. She explained that I was not only experiencing a miscarriage, but that it was a dangerous pregnancy known as an ectopic pregnancy, which is life-threatening to the woman.

I wasn't sure in that moment if I had heard her right. I asked her to repeat herself. I blinked, as if that would clear my thoughts and allow for more clarity on what was happening. She repeated herself very calmly and matter-of-factly as she watched me confusedly grasp what she was saying. At that moment, completely unsure of my intelligence, I looked at my husband, searching to know if I had heard her right. Was she informing us that my life was currently at high risk and might end if something wasn't done?

My husband took the lead and asked what that meant and how we could we ensure my safety. We were devastated. The day that was supposed to be the best day of our lives had turned out to be a living nightmare. Not only did we just learn that we were losing our baby, but my life was in danger and I could die if the medical emergency was not handled immediately. The one thing we wanted most was trying to kill me. I felt my heart being ripped out and shattered right before my very eyes. I just wanted it all to stop.

The nurse compassionately explained that we had to take precautionary measures immediately and terminate the pregnancy with a high dose of methotrexate. I sat there in disbelief as the nurse explained that she would be back with an assistant to administer the drug.

My husband was pacing as I cried. I could see his sadness grow and a fear rise when he looked at me. He was scared but kept calm as he expressed his concern and love for me. We had just received a blow of not only losing our baby, but now he could possibly lose me. It isn't a look that can be expressed in words. We cried, we held one another, and we waited and waited before the nurses stepped in the room to administer the methotrexate.

As they prepped the medication, I became numb and began isolating my mind from God. I was terrified and had no bravery within me at that moment. As I unbuckled my belt and unzipped my jeans to lower them, I raised my eyes to my husband, feeling confused and hurt. As the nurses began to prep the area above each hip where they would be giving me the shots, I asked Zach to hold me, knowing I needed him to be my physical support.

He took me in his arms without hesitation. As I wept, I cried out to the room, asking for confirmation that God has a plan over and over again. To my surprise, no one responded, and yet I begged the nurses to give me hope in that moment. As I held my husband, I fell deeper into him, allowing my weight to become his.

They gave me the shots, and as the drug burned into my body, I wrapped myself around my husband even tighter than I had ever before, while letting myself go. My heart sank deeper into the depths of despair and I wept. They placed a bandage on each side of my hips. I slowly raised my jeans, zipped them up and fastened my belt with red-stained eyes as they told me the next steps and precautions to take with the medication.

I don't remember much of what else was said that day, but it will always be burned into my memory as the worst day of my life. A day that was supposed to be full of hope became a day of tear-stained eyes and broken hearts. I wasn't sure how I would go on and how I would ever stand back up from the pain and sorrow I felt that September day.

My husband drove us home and as soon as we arrived, I knew I had to break the news to my dad, who was living with us. He didn't know I was pregnant and I was not sure how he would react. I told him that I had news to share and that he needed to sit down. He kept standing, so with desperation in my voice I asked him to sit down, as this was not good news. He slowly lowered himself onto the couch and I and my husband began letting the words fall calmly off our trembling lips. He sat quietly as the words began coming together. He listened. I could see my dad's heart sink for me. He showed a side of himself, full of empathy and emotion for his daughter whom he desperately loves, that I had never witnessed before. His eyes softened and he started to speak, asking what he needed to do to take care of his little girl and to make sure that my husband and I would be OK. My husband expressed his thankfulness for Dad's compassion and his understanding during this difficult time. I began to explain to my father that I was not sure about the next steps except that blood work was needed in the next week to ensure the medication did its job. Without hesitation, my father embraced me, and for a moment I felt a sense that all was going to be OK in that time of heartache and confusion. Not only did I have my loving husband, I also had my father to help me through this most difficult time.

Exhausted, sick, and ashamed that this was happening, I isolated myself to the confines of my bed and did my best to make the pain go away as I drifted to sleep.

The next day I had to work and try to hide the pain that consumed my every thought. When work was over a few hours later, my dad asked what precautions I needed to take to ensure my life was no longer in danger. He immediately opened his laptop and began looking for answers as I gathered the paperwork that was given to me a day prior listing all the precautions.

The documents that were given to me were so vague, confusing, and scary. As we gathered around his laptop and typed in the word "methotrexate" we held our breath. Seeing the explanation of the drug's effects was devastating, even though I knew that I didn't have a choice. My father and I scrolled the online documents for an explanation of what I should and should not do. How I should keep caution in the forefront and what foods to avoid. As the list went on, which seemed never-ending, I looked at the task as research, disconnecting myself from the severity and reality of the situation at hand.

It was easier that way. Easier in the sense that I could put my feelings on hold and do what I had to do. I was losing my baby and it wasn't as cut and dry or matter-of-fact as most people think. It would be a long, drawn-out, and agonizing process, and I honestly wanted to save my emotions. If I approached it as I did a bodybuilding competition and prepping my food, then wouldn't it be easier and less scary? I knew that weekly, I would have to walk into that clinic, lay out my arm and have them prick me as they drew my blood… the results confirming that my baby, who would never be, was slowly slipping further into heaven as my life would resume without that child in my life here on Earth, but who would be my guiding light in my heart.

I found peace knowing my baby would be with God, an angel in heaven protecting me from above.

As my father and I read the bold, black print on the screen, we began to make a list of what foods I should avoid. Looking at the list, my father and I realized it was everything I normally ate on multiple occasions throughout the day. Therefore, I called the nurse immediately, explaining how the list that was provided was vague and the research about foods to avoid was what I usually ate. The nurse kept telling me not to change my diet. However, all the research that had just consumed my morning begged to differ. I knew that in order for the methotrexate to work, I had to avoid these foods.

I learned a valuable lesson: that even though nurses and doctors are considered experts, I had to be my own advocate. The research proved to be right.

I posted the list on the fridge, changed my diet, modified my exercise, and braced myself for the weeks ahead.

With methotrexate and an ectopic pregnancy, you have to be monitored until there is no evidence of pregnancy within your bloodstream. I went in four days later and sat there numb and tearful as the prick of the needle reminded me once again I was losing my baby. They needed to make sure the beta level (of a hormone produced by the placenta during pregnancy) was decreasing. However, there was a chance it would still be increasing even with the first dose of methotrexate, which meant more would need to be given.

I received the call that afternoon to inform me that I needed to return for another treatment. We returned to the clinic that afternoon with even more sorrow in our hearts.

After that dose, I returned four days later and the results of my beta test were dropping. The new protocol was to return weekly for a painful reminder of our loss.

It took over 30 days to lose my baby. When I say losing, I mean for the beta, proof of pregnancy, to disappear. I didn't realize until I went through it that miscarriages are not immediate, at least not in my case. I not only had wounds on my heart, but I bled through the whole process, a daily reminder of no baby and the loss I was experiencing in silence.

As soon as the beta reached zero and no evidence of previous pregnancy existed, we regrouped with the doctor. We went over what had happened and the options before us. The only option that made sense was surgery. I was 36, with unexplained infertility, and now a history of ectopic pregnancy and unusual periods in my teenage years. Along with the mass that the ectopic pregnancy left behind, it only made sense to proceed to the operating room.

Before my surgery, I took a trip to Wyoming to see my best friend Jennifer and refresh my soul in the cold mountain air off the grid. It was what my heart needed. I was able to go into surgery with a clear mind and a calm heart in hopes of having a family someday.

Answers were found, and as they were revealed to me, I was in complete shock. The doctors found Stage 3 endometriosis, a polyp-covered uterus, and adhesions all within my abdominal cavity. I had had no idea. Not one clue. What a broken blessing that surgery turned out to be. The doctors found answers partially explaining my infertility. I never imagined my insides were a ticking time bomb of scar tissue, a uterus lined with miniature punching bags, and webs of adhesions all within my abdomen walls.

As I recovered, I asked how to prevent my body from reproducing these problems again and the doctor's response was, "Get pregnant!" If it was only that simple.

It is now June of 2019 and we are still working on it. I know God has a plan and I pray for patience daily, as I see His beauty within my life while gripping tightly to my hope, faith, and love for the life I have been blessed with. With infertility you can really start to lose who you are as a person and as a couple. We have decided to lift the pressure and take the summer off from doctor appointments, scheduling ultrasounds and blood work, and just get back to us.

With social media as a main source of information, it is hard to avoid controversial, unexplainable, as well as emotional discussions. There are those subjects that should be left well alone, such as politics, religion, sexuality, and — dare I say it — a woman's choice (yes, I am talking abortion and women's rights).

These topics sometimes end up in a nonsensical debate between strangers because they can't comprehend another's perspective or opinion. However, there are the subjects that touch one's heart, like a local hero who was just showing kindness, men stepping up when they didn't need to, and women suffering in silence.

Miscarriages or the loss of a child are topics that tug your heartstrings if you've been through it. If you haven't, then be glad for your heart's sake. Miscarriage is a "taboo" subject, just like a woman and her menstruation, domestic violence, and sexual assault. Those subjects, when brought up, are frowned upon; most of the time they are avoided and not talked about.

In my opinion, those are the very topics that need to be talked about — the elephants in the room. They need to be discussed so that many women feel accepted, understood, and shown compassion for their silenced suffering.

Now, a lot of people will have compassion for what I endured in the loss of my baby, and others will call me selfish and that I don't deserve kids. The fact is the baby would have never survived and if my body didn't have assistance in terminating the baby, I would have died. My miscarriage lasted weeks. I went in weekly to check my beta to make sure it was dropping and each time was more emotional than the last. You become numb to the prick of the needle and try to do your best to put a smile on while you fade into the background.

Many, far too many believe that they know what to say to a woman who has just experienced the greatest loss, a loss of her baby/child. To her it was her baby, and what will never be.

One day, I was scrolling through Facebook when I came across an article about miscarriages, titled "Studies acknowledge how traumatic miscarriage is — so why doesn't society?" by Anna O'Neil.[5]

I responded to the original post my friend had up on her wall and then I copied what I wrote and shared it to my wall, but privately, so I could remember it for my own healing.

I have advice for those who think they need to speak, to say something, and to those who avoid us because they don't know what to say. I hope this gives you some insight into how we are feeling, and that you

5 https://aleteia.org/2018/08/16/studies-acknowledge-how-traumatic-miscarriage-is-so-why-doesnt-society/

slowly begin to understand our pain. My response is as follows:

> Very spot on. I would like to add that regardless of the type of miscarriage, you can't compare them. They are all a loss that no one can understand unless they too have experienced it. A piece of you dies right along with that baby — it may be small or enormous... Either way, a hole is left. It is traumatic, and the worst of it all, is there was nothing we could as a mama-to-be do to protect that baby, so we blame ourselves, because we feel blame has to go somewhere, so why not take responsibility? People don't understand that! That was our baby and we are to protect it at all costs. Even the dad-to-be can suffer PTSD or depression from the loss. It's not because they feel responsible, but they hurt for their partner, lover, a best friend who had to also go through the loss and traumatic event of losing the baby not only emotionally, but physically, and there is and was nothing they could have done to protect them both. Preventing the loss of the baby and the events the mama has to go through.

It is a hard conversation to have regarding a miscarriage because no situation is the same, no back story is the same and there is no solution or words someone can give to help. We don't blame those who don't understand. We simply ask them to speak carefully and kindly. Those who are trying to help: you can't, you just can't. I know that if you simply let us grieve and take the time we need, we may be willing to talk about it and we may not, but it's ultimately our decision. However, the best thing one can do to help us that have suffered from a horrible and traumatic loss is to hug us a little tighter, love us a little deeper and just know silence may be what we need. It may allow us to hear the whisper of the lost soul we were given to be a mom to. A moment to remember the child we never got to hold, and a moment to just breathe while we grieve.

Miscarriage is a loss and we will never forget what could have been and we wouldn't want to no matter how deep it cuts into our heart and soul.

To all those who have loss, know it's OK not to be OK. Love to all of you and your angels.

I find peace in my response to the article, because it has allowed me to heal just a little more and it gives me comfort to know I have one more angel looking over me and my life. God needed my child more than I did, for reasons I will never know.

Infertility is definitely a battle that you are never prepared for, but once I found myself in the eye of this particular storm, I looked to God and took my husband's hand and held on tighter as we stepped into the unknown realities of it all.

Infertility has taught me a lot, and all I can say is that there is beauty in not being completely knowledgeable in the subject. However, I found that even the slightest whisper of the word and people turn away, not wanting any part of it. What a very twisted and lonely road a couple can experience together as they are surrounded by the idea of friends and family, but none seem to be in sight.

UNCONDITIONAL LOVE

Honey Baer

After everything my husband and I have been through, we are still deeply in love. I never knew what a marriage was supposed to look like. Sure, my mother was married for seven years to my former stepfather, but I was always playing outside or being creative and not really paying attention. In the summers I was with my father in California and most of the time he was single. I never really witnessed a happy marriage or what a couple in love looked like.

As I grew up I dreamt of being swept off my feet by Prince Charming, imagining the day I would marry my soulmate.

No one ever tells you that when you get married there is an *after*, after the happily ever after.

Life doesn't stop and become a fairytale ending after the "I do's." It becomes beautifully complicated.

There is now someone else in my life, one I chose to spend my days and nights with and to live this thing we are so blessed with, called life.

Another human being that I chose as my partner, to live, love, fight, and enjoy every day with. It's not written anywhere that life is guaranteed to be sunshine and rainbows. Because to have those, there must be clouds, rain, lightning, thunder and atrocious storms.

Without storms I wouldn't understand how truly blessed I am to have met and married the man I was meant to be with and to call my own.

Deeply in love, to walk through it all hand in hand, heart in heart as partners, lovers and best friends, while unconditionally loving each other, that is a marriage. I couldn't imagine what a marriage was supposed to be until I decided to be in this marriage.

My husband, my Honey Baer (yes, I spelled it correctly) has taught me so much about love, the unconditional kind. Over the course of our relationship he has been absolutely amazing even through the many tests life has thrown our way. Life is not fair; it's a complete rollercoaster within a complicated puzzle. However, there is no one else I would choose to do this life with by my side. It has been the most amazing thing I have ever experienced.

Getting married is a promise, a covenant that I have made to my husband, making the decision to share all the experiences — the good, bad, ugly, and complicatedly beautiful moments — with, hand in hand, side by side.

I'm not perfect, nor is my husband. However, we are each other's puzzle piece and we fit perfectly together. That is our perfect ending as one.

We have fought, bickered, argued, cried, yelled, laughed, smiled and experienced loss together, and loved through it all as a team.

We have jumped over small anthills and have conquered enormous mountains. We have fallen down and scraped our knees while climbing out of the depths of valleys. We have been through it all, not alone, but together.

I wouldn't change it, not for the world. Through debt and despair, to victories to loss, and confusion to growth and success, we have fallen more in love with each other with every passing day.

No one tells you life is hard; no one tells you marriage is hard. However, when I found myself doing this thing called life and doing it with my husband by my side, everything has been possible and the worst days have not broken us; they have only made us stronger.

Living life is one thing, but to live it fully in love with another is even more beautiful than one can imagine. That is unconditional love.

I would relive each and every challenge as if it were Groundhog Day, just to have one more day with my husband, who loves me — all of me — with all my baggage, quirky flaws, unlimited aspirations, and my goals to change the world.

My husband met me when I was just 26, broken and unworthy, but he saw something in me that told him I was the one. For me, I fell in love with his smile and his heart. I just knew I had to hold on to this one because he was made for me.

Our relationship moved fairly quickly for most outsiders looking in. For us it was the way God intended.

I didn't understand how this amazing man before me could ever be interested in the broken girl I found myself to be. He could have had anyone, yet he chose me. He fought for me against the lies I told myself about me. It took time, a long, long time before I stopped questioning his intentions with me. It took even longer for me to stop apologizing for everything, especially the broken baggage I kept lugging around, the person I was, and the person I was striving to be. He just accepted all of it. Told me that I am enough and I am loved.

Eventually, his patience, kindness, and unconditional love made a door for me to walk through. I then allowed myself to live authentically without fear of rejection. I slowly began seeing how truly amazing life could be, how awesome I have always been, while breaking the chains of my past.

He has never given up on me and to this day I am so thankful he is by my side cheering me on. My husband came into my life during my darkest year and he simply lit a candle so I wouldn't lose my way. He showed me that we could do this together and he has never left my side.

I love you, Honey Baer, for all that you are, for all that you do, and all our adventures: past, present and future. We vowed to each other over seven years ago to love one another unconditionally, and I plan to vow this to you every day until the end of time.

Unconditional love is one of those things that, when you find it, you never let go, never.

Chapter 6

Where I Am Now and How I Became My Own Hero

You may not control all the events that happen to you, but you can decide not to be reduced by them.
–Maya Angelou

If I had to wrap up or summarize my life, I would simply tell you it's been a beautiful journey of broken blessings that led me to become my own hero. I fortunately have had angels along the way as my guides to give me the gift of specific qualities I possess. I have been fortunate enough to pick up on the lessons I was taught to create the person I am today. Fairy tales are entertaining, feel-good stories that only exist in movies. For me, my journey gave me more than a happy ending, as my story isn't over. I may not have the Hollywood ending in some of my chapters and some are unfinished, which is OK, because it just means that chapter isn't over yet.

How can it be, I have just only begun?

As I finish this memoir, my infertility journey is still a storm I am in, my need for control still has a hold of my soul, and my desire to change the world one woman at a time is stronger than ever.

As I look back on the 36 years that I have been fortunate to live thus far, I am humbly thankful for all that I have been through. Some of it frightening, some of it enlightening, but all of it is a blessing.

If I had to do it all over again and I was given the option to change any of it, I can honestly say I wouldn't. I just hope I can do better with what has been laid out in front of me, realizing I have always been enough. Because at this point in my life, I am still learning the lessons I have been taught from adolescence to the present day.

I am still struggling with the baggage that I carry within my heart. I am still struggling with different areas in my life. And I am still hopeful that through it all I continue to learn the lessons that have been so willingly given to me as gifts from all those who cheered me on.

No one could save me; it wasn't their job. There were times I wondered why God would give me the battles He did and other times I was mad at Him for it all. However, I have learned that in all my trials, tribulations, glories, and wins I was always meant to be my own hero. It is not me being egotistical or full of myself; I am simply relying on the gifts God gave me, by placing all the blessings through people that I have been fortunate to meet and learn from along my path. We all have our path laid out in front of us, people who come and go within our lives, and the lessons that all the blessings teach us. It really is up to us, ourselves, to be our own heroes. To use the gifts that we possess and the ones that are given to us to create and write our story.

Through all my experiences and the people I was so blessed to have met, I learned the most valuable lessons, and I discovered I was my own hero all along. These people were my guiding lights and it was always up to me to find my own way. Without any one of them, I wouldn't be where I am today, and be the badass I am.

All the lessons can be summed up in one simple word: fortitude. I live my life with fortitude. Despite all that is thrown my way, I take it with grace and grit to find another success, even if I can't yet see it. I would rather live my life with a positive outlook in the midst of my storms than to be swept up and carried away by the deepest despair of all the storms I have been fortunate to survive. I am not saying it has been easy; however, it has been worth it.

I hope that I can keep on the passionate path that I have paved with so many angels who were right there alongside to help me. I hope that by telling my story, I inspire others to see how circumstances don't define you; rather they are your stepping stones that will lead you to live your life on your terms. It is ultimately a choice you have to make. I made the choice to take 100 percent responsibility for my life, and I have been rewarded tenfold.

Thank you, God, for giving me a desire to be an individual and seeking individuality at a young age.

Thank you, Mom, you showed me the meaning of acceptance for others as well as myself.

Thank you, Dad, for being an example of unquestionable strength.

Thank you, Mrs. Haney, for showing me the meaning of faith and how to hold on to it.

Thank you, Uncle Mario, for instilling in me that your pride is your own, and you must always remember that pride in yourself comes before all others.

Thank you, Dan and Rose, for showing me how to harness patience and to always seek it.

Thank you, Bob Kane, for showing me the power concentration can have on one's life.

Thank you, Dick Saatzer, for teaching me that integrity is our most valuable asset.

Thank you, Jennifer, my best friend, for your loyal friendship and showing me that a true friendship can and will last a lifetime.

Thank you, Tyler, my big brother, for spending all those summer days with me and teaching me what it means to have an unwavering passion and true tenacity.

Thank you, Verdugo Hills Golf Course, for giving me a place to call home. A place where I could discover who I was and who I was becoming while falling in love with golf. A place for many of the life lessons I learned. I mourn that you are no longer, but I cherish all the moments that were.

Thank you, Coach Cap, for encouraging me to find determination for whatever I desire, even when it seems impossible.

Thank you, Dr. Darden, for showing me how to harness the desire for growth. Without that I would still be the scared little girl curled up in the blue chair.

Thank you, Rich, for teaching me to harness courage and how to never let people forget who I am.

Thank you to the Tipping Point; without the lesson of abuse I might have stayed in that relationship for too long and not be here today.

Thank you, Coach KP, for believing in me and helping me connect my relentless need for control and turn it into self-discipline.

Thank you to the Accident I endured that allowed me to seek mindfulness.

Thank you, Coach LeAnn, for showing me that as long as I had persistence, I could accomplish anything, even with everything against me.

Thank you, Zach Baer — my Honey Baer — for always loving me unconditionally through it all; my faults, my insecurities, my successes and my failures, and allowing me to always pursue my dreams to make a difference in the world. Without you, I would be lost.

Chapter 7

Always Be Your Own Hero

Keep your eyes on the vision, you won't lose your way.
–Erin Baer

TENACITY

April 29, 2019

The eyes of a woman are a complicated, beautiful force
When you take a moment to look into the eyes of a woman
First you will see the color within
Look harder, you see our light that shines through
Look farther, the beauty that encompasses our life
Look longer, the darkness that surrounds us
Look beyond the darkness, you see our pain
Look into the pain and you discover our soul
Our soul holds our truth, secrets and vulnerability within
our world
Our vulnerability is our courage
Our courage reveals our strength
Don't dismiss your chance to witness such wonder

The best advice I can give you is to grab onto the hope in my story and never let it go. Look into yourself and you will find that you have the strength to unleash the badass in you. It has been there all along. You may feel defeated and feel life is unfair. However, the only way you lose is if you don't learn and you don't get back up.

Life is a gift we have all been given. Life was never promised to be easy; in fact if it was, I wouldn't be writing this book to give you hope and strength. I wouldn't need to, as there would not be any stories that would need to be told because it would have been all rainbows and butterflies.

Life is messy; it's complicated and undeniably hard, yet I wouldn't have it any other way. It makes the fight worth it; it makes getting up that much easier with each blow. All in all life is uniquely, imperfectly perfect. It's your life and you can live your life on your terms. You just have to know you're worth it. You're enough and you're a badass.

THE END

OR, IS THIS JUST THE BEGINNING?

LIVE AND LOVE EVERY MOMENT

October 2, 2001

As a sunrise starts a new day, a birth starts a new life
As water creates, it can take it all away
Even though it happens every day,
It has its purpose
Its story
Its own beginning

Life has so many meanings to each and everything
Its own way of traveling down the path of roughness, while
smoothing out the wrinkles

Life is so amazing as long as you try
It is worth living, and seeking is so incredible

If it's worth believing in not everything, but the most
important thing
Many don't know and how could they if they didn't
understand themselves

They need to love not just themselves,
But to love everything about their souls
All have themselves to live for in their divine way

They've created dreams and set goals
One must not breathe one must take a breath
For it's the secret that allows the heart to feel pain, joy and
sadness

Life is not about what to do, but how to do it
It doesn't matter who you meet or who you don't it's about
what you do when you meet them

Beauty is not just a word, nor is it just visual, but it is physical
It is a feeling one does not learn; it is known if you want to feel it

Everything always seems as if it must be learned, but the truth is we know, but do we want to admit it was there all along or are we scared to live? Truly live?

One in order to live must give up the principle behind justice and give into emotional attachment
Because if you allow barriers to stop you, your heart will die

Because you didn't accept failure while looking for comfort within your purpose

It's not hard it's just inconvenient for people to understand
It doesn't come overnight it's there always because remember you're alive
You are here

But the mystery is not far, because you have the power to live
Not for them, but for you and him Almighty God

When you leave the physical world, you are saying
You made it through
You are not saying Goodbye
You're just saying I'll see you on the other side

Until then… live

Resources

National Domestic Violence Hotline

- 1-800-799-7233
- https://www.thehotline.org/

Beaten to Badass

- To learn more about empowering yourself and others and to support the organization, see https://beatentobadass.com

Zero Tolerance for Domestic Abuse

- For information on this Colorado-based organization, see https://0t4da.org/

In Gratitude

Thank you to:

Zach Baer, the love of my life, who has unconditionally loved me, supported me and motivates me to live my life with purpose and intention every single day.

Lauren Danielle, who I instantly connected with from the first moment we met, for giving me the courage to finish my story and who has continued to cheer me on to live an inspired life.

Amy Collette, who from the moment I met immediately encouraged me that my story was worth sharing with the world and shouldn't be hidden. Who has guided and coached me to tell it from my viewpoint and has helped me deliver it in such a way that everyone will see themselves in the pages of my story.

Melody Christian, my cover designer who was able to capture the essence of who I am and what I represent in a simple yet elegant way what being a Badass is all about.

All the women who have given me hope and inspiration by sharing their stories with me and encouraged me to do the same.

To all my clients who have inspired and motivated me every day, who are more my family, I love you all.

To my family and friends. Without you, I wouldn't be who I am today, and for that I am forever thankful.

About the Author

Erin Baer is the founder of the organization Beaten to Badass. As a survivor of domestic violence and sexual assault, she began telling her story of grace and grit. Raped, beaten, nearly killed, bullied, abandoned, abused, and broken... She shouldn't have survived, but she did. Erin's story began giving other women the strength, hope, and courage to keep going and become the BADASS they were always meant to be.

Seeing women being silenced for wanting to be strong, courageous, and proud of who they are while moving on from feeling beaten down in life, Erin decided to be the voice to stand up for those women, to show them that their circumstances don't define them, and that they too can be their own heroes. A portion of every sale of *From Beaten to Badass* goes back to those impacted by domestic violence and sexual assault.

Erin holds a BSBA in Business Administration from Rockhurst University and an MBA in Business Management from Avila University. Erin enjoys her work as an Empowerment Coach, Personal Trainer, and Golf Professional. She lives in Colorado with her husband, Zach.

Connect with Erin

Beatentobadass.com
Facebook: beatentobadass
Instagram: beatentobadass
LinkedIn: erinbaerbadass

Made in the USA
Columbia, SC
27 June 2020

12287320R00128